Tell me a Story

WHY STORIES ARE ESSENTIAL TO EFFECTIVE SAFETY TRAINING

REPORT OF INVESTIGATIONS 9664

ELAINE T. CULLEN, Ph.D., and
ALBERT H. FEIN, Ph.D.

NIOSH
National Institute for
Occupational Safety and Health

Tell me a Story

WHY STORIES ARE ESSENTIAL TO EFFECTIVE SAFETY TRAINING

REPORT OF INVESTIGATIONS 9664

ELAINE T. CULLEN, Ph.D., and
ALBERT H. FEIN, Ph.D.

August 2005

Disclaimer Page

Ordering Information

To receive documents or more information about
occupational safety and health topics, contact NIOSH at:

NIOSH -- Publications Dissemination
4676 Columbia Parkway
Cincinnati, OH 45226-1998

Telephone: 1-800-35-NIOSH (1-800-356-4674)
Fax: 513-533-8573
E-mail: Pubstaft@cdc.gov

or visit the NIOSH Web site at www.cdc.gov/niosh

SAFER•HEALTHIER•PEOPLE ™

DHHS (NIOSH) Publication No. 2005-152
August 2005

Acknowledgments

A work such as this owes more than I can say to the many miners across the West who have cheerfully and enthusiastically assisted me in filming, acting, evaluating, and encouraging the production of these videos. They have opened their hearts and their souls to recall painful memories of one of the most frightening experiences that can happen to a miner–a mine fire. They have given time and thoughtful consideration of what a new miner needs to know to survive in a work environment noted for its dangers and its harshness. Photographs of some of them are scattered throughout this document.

In addition, I want to acknowledge the contribution of the professional film crew from TCI/ComCast who worked with us on this research effort. Diane Cortez, production manager, Brian Headding, editor, Bill Fitzner and Ann Byers, videographers, made these videos a reality with their willingness to try a sometimes frighteningly unknown environment, their enthusiasm in adjusting to mining schedules and culture, and the good humor that they conveyed to the miner-actors as they encouraged them and coached them through the filming of the videos. Their patience and professionalism were much appreciated. I also appreciate the contributions of my co-author, Dr. Albert Fein, Associate Professor at Gonzaga University. The work he did on the evaluation of the effectiveness of our training videos was both professional and invaluable. Thanks also go to the two who helped format this publication, Priscilla Wopat, technical editor, and Kim Clough-Thomas, visual information specialist. It may take a village to raise a child, but this publication shows that it takes a village to tell a good story!

Elaine T. Cullen, Ph.D.

Table of Contents

List of Figures

Tell me a Story

WHY STORIES ARE ESSENTIAL TO EFFECTIVE SAFETY TRAINING

Elaine T. Cullen, Ph.D.[1]
Albert H. Fein, Ph.D.[2]

ABSTRACT

Federal law mandates that all miners receive safety and health training when first entering the mining industry and at least 8 hours annually thereafter. Although the mining industry has historically relied on an experiential master-apprentice model for training new employees, the formal safety training provided to miners is generally done in a classroom, with mixed results. In a series of stakeholder meetings held by NIOSH across the West in 1997-2000, trainers identified significant gaps in materials that were available to teach new and experienced miners. They asked whether NIOSH could develop effective materials to fill these perceived gaps, as well as make training more effective for those who were required to attend, but who often refused to be attentive. Adult learning theories, social learning theories, mentoring, and storytelling were all employed in the development of a series of safety training videos that have become very popular in the mining industry. This Report of Investigations describes the theoretical frameworks that were used, the process that was developed to produce the videos, and the results of the evaluations as to whether or not they were effective in training new and experienced miners.

[1] Communications chief, Spokane Research Laboratory, National Institute for Occupational Safety and Health, Spokane, WA.
[2] Associate professor, Gonzaga University, Spokane, WA.

8

INTRODUCTION

Since 1977, when the Mine Safety and Health Act was revised to include U.S. metal and nonmetal mines in addition to coal mines, safety training for all mine workers has been legislatively mandated. Under the Act, new underground miners are required to receive a minimum of 40 hours of training before beginning their careers, and incoming surface miners are required to receive 24 hours. Thereafter, every employee is required to attend a minimum of 8 hours of annual refresher training that is to include discussions of safety and health as well as information on hazard recognition and other topics deemed necessary by mine management and the Mine Safety and Health Administration (MSHA).

In late 1998, NIOSH funded a small-scale research project at its Spokane Research Laboratory (SRL) entitled "Development and Evaluation of Effective Safety Training for Miners." This project was initiated in response to requests heard during a series of stakeholder meetings held by SRL staff around the West. At these meetings, mine safety professionals reported what they perceived to be a critical lack of appropriate materials that could be used to train both new and experienced miners. They observed that for many topics, the only materials available were decades old and, in some cases, were outdated enough to make them irrelevant. The safety trainers were in agreement that these materials were ineffective at best and that miners both dreaded and resisted the federally mandated safety training because they considered it a waste of time. Thus, while the law was specific in its requirement that miners attend training, it could not mandate that miners learn.

The principal investigator (the primary author) on this project gathered a group of safety trainers and directors from operating mines throughout the West to assist in the selection of topics, methods, and training media so that the resulting training materials would be both useful to and used by industry trainers. Concurrently, research began on adult and social learning theories, training methods, effects of culture on learning, and best practices in occupational training. Because video was the medium preferred by members of the advisory group, all products developed under the project were in the form of videotapes.

When completed, reviewed, and released, the videos created were provided free of charge to mine safety professionals. A database was generated that included the customers[3] who requested videos; this database allowed information to be gathered on how and when the videos

[3] Because most of the trainers who received the videos were employed in Western underground mines, this group composed the largest demographic subgroup during the evaluation phase of the project.

were used. Evaluators incorporated data from miners who had viewed the training videos and from trainers who had shown the videos in training sessions to determine how the videos were being used and whether or not they were truly effective.

This Report of Investigations discusses the first seven videos produced as part of the project, the theoretical models used in creating the videos, the methods used to produce them, and an evaluation of their effectiveness as determined by the miners and safety trainers. Six training videos dealt with underground mining, in particular, underground hard-rock

mining. Although the topics covered (which include ground control methods, working with explosives, and recognition of roof and mobile equipment hazards) are common to most underground mines, unlike older training films, these videos were all shot in deep hard-rock mines using real hard-rock miners as actors. The seventh video, *You Are My Sunshine*, describes the events leading up to the disastrous Sunshine Mine fire of 1972 and the lessons learned from it; the story of the fire is told through the experiences and voices of 27 people who lived through it.

REVIEW OF RELEVANT THEORETICAL FRAMEWORKS

By Elaine T. Cullen

Miners are not considered to be traditional learners. Their work is physical and is performed in an environment frequently described as hostile. Survival in this environment depends on the ability to maintain a constant state of awareness about potential dangers, to read the signs of danger and make sense of what's happening, and to react appropriately when the environment changes. Kowalski-Trakofler et al. (2004, p. 2) state that —

Training is especially relevant in the mining industry because the mine environment is dynamic and constantly changing. This dynamic environment makes engineering controls harder to implement and frequently less effective than they might be on a shop floor.

Although federal law requires miners to attend safety training classes, in reality, these workers tend to learn their trade in a mine, not in a classroom, and they generally learn from more-experienced miners in a master-apprentice relationship rather than from reading training manuals or safety policies and regulations. New miners coming into the industry belong to demographic cohorts that do not expect to be taught in a traditional, authoritative classroom setting (Kowalski-Trakofler et al., p. 5). The miners themselves are very explicit about how they prefer to learn—

It's on-the-job training. They would never put you with an inexperienced person, they'd put you with one who was already experienced. And you'd learn your trade through that person. He'd teach you what he knows and then maybe a few weeks or months down the road you might partner up with another individual that also has several years of training and he'll teach you his methods of work and so forth. (Mitchell, personal communication, 2001)

You don't want to...[learn to mine] with somebody you don't trust and don't look up to. And I think that's why...everybody will name somebody that taught them, you know, because...he was willing to take time and show these guys how to survive, really. That's what they are teaching them is how to survive....There's no way that you can learn that in a classroom. You've got to be down there one-on-one with a miner....You ain't gonna learn nothing until you get down there and actually start doing it. (Jerome, personal communication, 2002)

Federal law, however, requires that new hires *participate* in a classroom course, and typically the trainer generally relies on a traditional "I talk, you listen" model. One of the primary goals of the project research, therefore, was to find alternate ways to provide information and training to miners that would be effective in both keeping

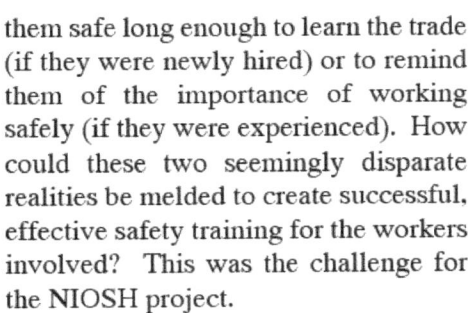

them safe long enough to learn the trade (if they were newly hired) or to remind them of the importance of working safely (if they were experienced). How could these two seemingly disparate realities be melded to create successful, effective safety training for the workers involved? This was the challenge for the NIOSH project.

Adult Learning Styles

Theories of Adult Learning

Miners fit the definition of "adult learners" as described by Knowles, Holton, and Swanson (1998). As adult learners, they make decisions about what, or indeed, even whether, they choose to learn. Knowles, who is generally credited with being one of the originators of modern adult learning theory, based his theory on primary assumptions about how adults learn. These include the need for training to be grounded in real-life experiences and the premise that skills or knowledge learned must be applicable to immediate circumstances. Adults are pragmatic in their learning. Unlike children in a schoolroom, they will not put energy into learning what does not appear relevant to their lives. For training to be effective, adult learners—

- Need to know why they need to learn something.
- Need training to be self-directed.
- Need training to be related to prior experience.
- Must be ready to learn.
- Must be motivated to learn.
- Must believe that what they are learning is oriented toward problem solving. (pp. 64-68)

Adults are motivated to learn those things that will be helpful in solving problems or will provide what Knowles calls an "internal payoff" rather than an external one (p. 149). While this does not mean that adults don't value promotions or pay raises that may result from increased training, the stronger motivator is the satisfaction of perceived internal needs. Knowles (p. 149) cites Wlodowski (1985) in explaining this preference, who suggests that adult learners are more motivated to learn if—

- They believe they will be successful.
- They believe they have a choice in whether or not to learn.
- They see the training as valuable.

Caudron (2000) interviewed a number of adult professionals to gather information on what effective training looked like. Responses from participants were consistent and showed that adults learn differently than do children. Their most memorable learning came from personal experiences, from working within groups of other adult learners, and from mentoring they received from someone they perceived to be both knowledgeable and wise.

Caudron also discovered that in spite of this preference for real-world training, over 70% of current training in organizations was still the talking-head variety, with a trainer in front of a classroom and the trainees sitting and listening passively. While this may be an effective way to teach children, it doesn't work well with adults. It's no wonder that trainees are impatient with this type of training. Not only is it NOT self-directed or experiential, it's not very interesting. Trainers who are required to teach a range of technical topics but who don't make classes enjoyable are missing the boat, according to Owenby, who states, "Training programs that deal strictly with technical, job-related subjects are boring" (1992, p. 43).

An investigation into theories of adult learning and occupational training revealed many to choose from, and they often included differing objectives or ideas. Zemke suggests that there is no such thing as an overall "general theory of adult learning" (2002, p. 89). He believes that all have valid points to make, but for any training to be truly effective, it is necessary to choose the theoretical framework that best fits the trainees themselves as well as the organization's training objectives and its occupational culture. The goal is not necessarily to increase knowledge, but rather to create expertise.

Social learning theory (SLT) may provide the best model for the creation of training materials for skilled blue-collar workers, particularly those who work in trades that depend on older, wiser workers to mentor new employees, as mining does. SLT has its roots in theories of behaviorism originally described by Skinner and other psychologists in the 1940's in which rewards and punishments were considered to have a great impact on behavior. SLT was officially proposed by two researchers, Miller and Dollard, as a means of explaining human behavior. Their book, *Social Learning and Imitation*, was published in 1941 (Stone, 1999), and in the ensuing years, many other researchers have refined or redefined different aspects of the original theory.

Bandura is an accepted leader in the field of social learning theory, or, as he calls it, social cognitive theory (Miller, 1993, pp. 192-195). Bandura suggests that people learn not only by personal experiences, but also by watching the experiences of others, which he terms "vicarious learning." This hypothesis has strong relevance to the development of effective training materials, for if proper role models or mentors can be convinced to share their experiences, their stories will provide valuable learning opportunities.

The common tenet of existing social learning theories is that an individual's behavior is influenced by observing the behaviors of others, particularly people who are admired or viewed as mentors, teachers, coaches, etc. Humans are a species that learns by watching others, but imitation of others' behavior is more likely to occur if the mentor possesses characteristics that the learner views as desirable and if the mentor is similar to the learner. In addition, the behaviors that are modeled must be seen as constructive by the learner, with a positive impact, or the behavior will be avoided instead of imitated (Zemke, 2002).

Relevance of Adult Learning Theory to Training

Perhaps the most compelling reason for providing training is to try to change people's behavior in some fashion. This is especially true in safety training. Stone (1999, p. 3) states that the primary purpose of the various social learning theories is—

- To understand and predict individual and group behavior and
- To identify methods in which behavior can be modified and changed.

Stone further states that SLT is frequently used by public health specialists because of its applicability to changing the behaviors and beliefs of individuals toward adopting healthier or safer choices. Clearly there is value to safety trainers and developers of safety training materials in understanding why people make unsafe choices and in identifying ways to influence those choices toward safer ones. Under this theory, the key is to provide appropriate role models from whom to learn: people who are respected, admired, and who have credibility. For these role models to be most effective, their experiences must be relevant to the learning expected and tied to the work experience and culture of the learners.

Kowalski and Vaught state that adult learners "learn best by having [their own] experiences and reflecting on them" (2002, pp. 3-4), but Bandura would add that adults can also learn by reflecting upon the experiences of others. Bandura's concept of the strength of vicarious learning becomes even more significant when considering that, in the mining industry, many of the experiences shared by mentors are descriptions of close calls or are stories about people they have known who were injured or killed on the job. Sharing such histories is an integral part of the oral tradition of the mining culture; it is hoped that new miners will avoid such close calls and learn the lessons simply by hearing about them. For miners working in potentially dangerous environments, this can mean the difference between working safely and being injured or even killed. It is imperative that training be "effective," but this can be an elusive goal.

Zemke (2002) states that four separate processes must occur if effective observational learning is going to occur.

1. The learner must pay attention to what's happening.

2. He or she must remember what was seen.

3. He or she must be physically and intellectually capable of mimicking the behavior.

4. He or she must have the motivation or reinforcement to model it.

In an environment that relies heavily on master-apprentice learning, as does the mining industry, these processes may be the keys to effective training.

Mentors

The importance of a mentor in developing safe, productive workers cannot be overstated. Many researchers have identified mentoring as a key component to effective learning, particularly in those hands-on trades that require a high degree of skill in performing work tasks and a sensitivity to potential or real hazards. Darwin says, "For centuries, mentoring has been used as a vehicle for handing down knowledge, maintaining culture, supporting talent, and securing future leadership" (2000, p. 197).

Camm and Cullen (2002) discuss the value of mentoring new hires and provide an overview of prevailing theories about why mentoring works particularly well in skilled blue-collar occupations. Pegg (1999) attributes mentors' credibility as expert teachers to many things, including their financial and occupational successes, perceived street smarts about how to survive, personal presence or charisma, or simply their age and length of experience. No matter where the source of their credibility lies, however, it is true that good mentors are admired and trusted and that they play key roles in training and teaching new employees.

Lucas (1969) provides a view of how the social relationships between mentors and apprentices develop, particularly in mining communities, and discusses why they are so effective. It is his belief that young people are enculturated at a very early age. They grow up hearing stories about what happens in the mines and about the people, usually men, who are working there. They see for themselves the "toys" that top miners can afford, and the community's young men develop a natural desire to be like them. They admire the economic and social position that good miners have in the community and in the mining culture itself.

In mining communities that are geographically isolated and provide a minimum of good-paying jobs, young people have few choices other than mining if they want to stay in the area. Thus, by the time they are old enough to work in the mines, they are ready to join that unique occupational culture, knowing that they will be taught and protected by someone who knows the ropes (Lucus, 1969).

McCarl adds that the status of a mentor or master miner is directly tied to his experiences underground and how he handled them. "A man's skill performances below ground, particularly during times of stress or danger, are by far the most important media through which his identity and reputation are created" (1997, p. 13). Miners know who is admired and understand clearly who would be both their best teacher and their best chance of survival should disaster strike. These masters are generally informal leaders, but they are also mentors to anyone wanting to learn their lessons without having to experience directly the incidents that taught those lessons.

A good mentor is seen as a truth teller, as one who will provide an honest picture of what is happening. To an inexperienced person, unsure of what to do and how to survive, this is invaluable. Voynick (1978) describes his own apprenticeship as a new miner and remembers that the old hands provided many valuable lessons in subtle and not-so-subtle ways. Young hands may learn from any other miner, but most often, their practical training is entrusted to an assigned mentor—a journeyman miner who teaches in three essential areas:

- Knowledge about what's important

  Knowledge about how to do things right

- Knowledge about the culture, including the values and attitudes expected if one is to take one's place in the occupational culture (Billett, 1994).

Expert miners have the credibility and the position within the mining culture to be taken seriously as trainers and teachers. Gargiulo provides this insight into the role played by expert mentors. "Learning results from piecing together our experiences. One experience builds on another….Experts have more experience; and whether they realize it or not, they apply that experience to novel situations" (2002, p. 35). The ability to use what one knows (the knowledge) when facing a new or unusual situation is one way to describe wisdom, and these master miners have earned their wisdom through hard experiences. Mentors, then, have a powerful role to play in the training of new employees as they share their stories, their experiences, their knowledge, and their wisdom.

Role of Culture

If training materials are going to be truly successful, they must not only include accurate and relevant content, but must also work seamlessly within the culture the trainers seek to influence, or they will face the resistance that the members of that culture will exhibit. Culture is a difficult thing to identify, but can be simply explained as "the way we do things around here." It effectively defines what is acceptable and what is not.

Hofstede defines culture as "the collective programming of the mind which distinguishes the members of one group or category of people from another" (1997, p. 5). Patton believes that culture provides the road map by which members of that culture negotiate the world.

> Culture is that collection of behavior patterns and beliefs that constitutes standards for deciding what is, standards for deciding how one feels about it, standards for deciding what to do about it, and standards for deciding how to go about doing it. (2002, p. 81)

Van Maanen and Barley further the argument by suggesting the existence of "occupational communities" (or occupational cultures), which they define as—

> A group of people who consider themselves to be engaged in the same sort of work; whose identity is drawn from the work; who share with one another a set of values, norms and perspectives that apply to but extend beyond work-

related matters; and whose social relationships meld work and leisure. (1984, p. 287)

If occupational culture is a gatekeeper that provides its members with guidelines on what to do and how to do it, then it is also the primary key to successfully changing their behaviors. Occupational cultures that are particularly strong because of shared dangers faced by their members (such as police, firefighters, loggers, or miners) will be very resistant to changes suggested by outsiders. However, if these changes are recommended and accepted by insiders, they are much more likely to be adopted.

Danger...invites work involvement and a sense of fraternity....Recognition that one's work entails danger heightens the contrast between one's own work and the safer work of others, and encourages comparison of self with those who share one's work situation. Attitudes, behaviors, and self-images for coping physically and psychologically with threat become part of an occupational role appreciated best, it is thought, only by one's fellow workers. (Van Maanen & Barley, 1984, p. 301)

The term "occupational culture" is very applicable to miners. Their identity is strongly tied to their work, and they can be distrustful of outsiders, especially those who come into their environment and try to tell them how to do their work. Van Maanen and Barley believe that occupational communities such as mining

use task rituals, behavioral norms, work codes, and stories to reinforce the values and standards expected from members, and that this will be most prevalent in "those occupations that transmit a shared culture from generation to generation of participants" (1984, p. 292). In an occupation such as mining, culture can be seen as both a strength, as expected norms and values have developed over many years and are well-grounded in practical experience, or as a hindrance to changing aspects that are antithetical to safety or health.

Occupational culture must be considered when dealing with any attempt to change behaviors within it. Schein admits that early social researchers failed to appreciate its power and did not see that "culture, viewed as such taken-for-granted, shared, tacit ways of perceiving, thinking, and reacting, was one of the most

powerful and stable forces operating" (1996, p. 232). Hansen suggests that new information provided to people (through training, for example) will always be filtered through the beliefs, experiences, and norms provided by their occupational culture. Because members of an occupational culture believe that "members have the exclusive right to perform a given set of related tasks," they can be resistant to outside influences (1995, p. 60). Hansen ties learning directly to the norms and traditions of the work culture and states that "information communicated in a manner greatly different from what is culturally common requires a longer learning period and often leads to a lack of comprehension or misunderstanding" (p. 61).

The value of using peer trainers, or people who are inside an occupational culture and know its ways and its language, is apparent. Because they are "members of the tribe," these people have the ability to break through the barriers created by a culture that is resistant to outside influence. They understand the norms, values, semiotics, and unwritten rules that govern the culture and can maneuver successfully through them.

Kowalski and Vaught state that adults "come to the learning situation from a particular environment and with a personal history" (2002, p. 4). While more traditional training theories focus on the skills and abilities of individuals, current belief is that the environment (which likely includes occupational culture) and the dynamics existing within the training group play important roles in effective learning. Adults come to training classes as experts in some area, and this expertise, according to Kowalski and Vaught, needs to be recognized and honored. This is congruent with what other scholars have said, that learning is an interactive process for adults and that the culture is used by learners to determine what is important and what is not.

One of the most basic components of effective training is the language (jargon) used by a trainer. Hansen (1995) acknowledges that occupational cultures often develop their own distinct jargon that communicates what is important to members, as well as members' perceptions of that information. Jargon has the added benefit of excluding nonmembers, who may not understand the meaning of terms or constructs. Thus, understanding and using accepted occupational jargon are critical to a trainer's success.

"People...feel more comfortable and trusting of those who are most like themselves" (Hansen, 1995, p. 62). The federal government recognizes this factor and in regulations pertaining to mine safety training, states that "You must ensure that each program, course of instruction, or training session is...presented in language understood by the miners who are receiving the training" (U.S. Code of Federal Regulations, 30 46.4(3), 2001). One might argue that it was the intent of the authors of this regulation to assure that non-English speakers be trained in their native tongue, but it clearly also speaks to the need to communicate effectively to every miner by using language that is understood by him or her. This would mean using occupational jargon—the tribal language—of mining when developing any training. Creating these materials in bureaucratic or highly technical language not commonly used by the miners themselves would increase the likelihood that the regulations and materials will be ignored.

Value of Storytelling

Humans are storytellers. Stories have been used throughout history to entertain, to inform, to provide a sense of inclusiveness in the narrative of mankind. Stories work at a very different level than pure information-sharing because they deal not just with rational thought, but also with how we feel about what we have heard. Stories are able to move beyond the barriers people create, to touch not just our minds, but our hearts.

Trying to change another person's behavior permanently (one of the primary objectives of safety training) without obtaining their buy-in is impossible. It is true that people will change their behaviors to generally comply with mandated rules when they must (when the supervisor or the inspector is watching, for example), but when nobody is around to monitor their behavior, they often revert to how things have always been done and how their occupational culture expects them to behave, particularly if those mandates are in conflict with culturally expected behaviors. To openly go up against a traditional norm, people have to be convinced that the new behavior is a better choice and that the choice to follow it is their choice.

The key for a safety trainer, then, is to find the internal control switch in each trainee that responds to the "why should I care about this information?" question and provides the answer "because it makes sense for me to care. It may save my life some day." Stories have the ability to do this.

Gargiulo suggests that stories have many uses. While it is true that stories evoke different memories and responses in different people (generally depending on individual experiences and values), Gargiulo states flatly that "The hallmark of intelligence is our ability to collect stories and regularly reflect on them in order to gain new insights from them" (2002, p. 6).

The roles played by stories are numerous. Among them, Gargiulo lists the following:

- Stories empower the speaker.
- Stories create an environment of trust.
- Stories create a bond among those who hear them.
- Stories engage the mind.
- Stories have a unique ability to defuse conflict and differences of opinion.
- Stories encode a lot of cultural information.
- Stories provide a way to learn from personal or vicarious experiences.
- Stories can be used as weapons.
- Stories bring about healing. (pp. 7-37)

Slater has studied the immense power that stories have. He claims that stories—

have substantial potential to influence behavior. It is difficult to consider another communication genre that can communicate beliefs, model behavior, teach skills, provide behavioral cues, and simulate consequences of behaviors over time in as compelling a fashion. (2002, p. 16)

Simmons believes that stories are "the oldest tool of influence in human history" (2001, p. xvii) and that they can provide the trainer with an effective way to "connect people to what's important and to help them make sense of their world" (p. 29). In other words, stories have the power to provide the answer to the critical question "why should I care about what this teacher/trainer is saying?"

Stories have been recognized by many organizational theorists for their power to communicate not only information, but also the culture of an organization. Zemke states that stories "can act as powerful directives for members' behavior, and they can teach specific lessons as well" (1990, p. 44). As such, they can provide the "culture map" that guides new employees and point out "the dangerous and the safe" (p. 45). In a work environment, stories provide both the philosophy of an organization in a way that inspires those coming into it and enough information about what to do and how to act once they are inspired to do something. Good training stories will thus provide information on what to do, as well as how to do it, why it is important to do it "this way," and what

the consequences may be for ignoring the established norms.

Lave and Wenger (1991) argue that true learning does not take place in isolation, but rather in a socially interactive environment. Stories are inherently social. They entertain, but they also show what others would do in a given environment when faced with a certain set of circumstances. Those watching or hearing stories of this type are drawn into the tale. They associate with the characters, and by placing themselves vicariously into the scenario, they can investigate how they would feel or behave in similar circumstances.

The benefits of vicariously experiencing dangerous or harmful environments or incidents are obvious. Learning can take place while the learner remains safe. Bruner believes that it is only through interaction with others in the context of a specific culture that we can find meaning and understanding of our world. "Human beings…are expressions of a culture. To treat the

world as an indifferent flow of information to be processed by individuals each on his or her own terms is to lose sight of how individuals are formed and how they function" (1990, p. 12). Geertz sums this view up by stating "There is no such thing as human nature independent of culture" (1973, p. 49). Stories are effective in connecting us to the experiences of others, to those who are telling the stories, and more broadly, to the overall culture in which the stories exist. It is not necessary to repeat the experiences, then, in order to learn from them.

Storytelling is often associated with entertaining or teaching children, but MacDonald believes that **"The adult's sense of story is fully developed, the attention span is long, and adults provide eager listeners if you will take the time to seek out...tales we need to hear"** (1993, p. 57). The love of stories is not lost when people grow up. In fact, it may be that adults are better listeners than the young.

Training is only effective when the trainer is able to connect with learners and provide lessons that are perceived by them as valuable. Stories provide a powerful tool to do this, and as Wylie says, they "make the important interesting" (1998, p. 30). Trainees, especially those new to an industry, are often bombarded with a bewildering amount of new information, much of it as unfamiliar as the environmental or occupational landscape. It is a daunting task to organize and make sense of this information, much less to remember it long enough to put it into action.

In the opinion of King and Down (2001), it is the hope (perhaps the goal) of trainers and teachers that learners will take the information provided to them, turn it into knowledge of their task or occupation, and eventually reach understanding of when and how to apply that knowledge. This is what the expert mentor does as a matter of habit.

'Story' is a way of knowing and remembering information—a shape or pattern into which information can be arranged. It serves a very basic purpose; it restructures experiences for the purpose of 'saving' them. And it is an ancient, perhaps natural order of mind....By imposing the structure of a story onto some circumstance or happening, greater coherence and sensibility are achieved within the event itself, and otherwise isolated and disconnected scraps are bound up into something whole and meaningful. (Livo & Rietz, 1986, p. 5)

King and Down (2001) believe that one of the simplest functions of stories is that they provide us with a way to better remember information. People, they argue, pay attention and listen more attentively to stories. If paying attention and remembering what has been told are two keys to effective learning, as Zemke (2002) argues, then stories make learning not only possible, but increase the likelihood that people will learn. Forster et al. sum it up by stating that—

> Stories...act as both mirrors and windows on the human experience, showing people either how to look at reality in a different way or suggesting alternative realities.... Traditions of storytelling have enabled human beings to make sense of the world that surrounds them, and their place in it, for millennia. (1999, pp. 11-12)

putting confusing information into a more understandable context.

Neuhauser discusses the different levels of consciousness that stories access and why this aspect of theirs is valuable in a learning environment.

Changing the voluntary behavior of adults is not a simple task. Cranton (1994) believes that "transformational learning" (the primary objective of safety training—to truly change the belief system and subsequently the behavior of workers) is the key. True transformational learning occurs through critical self-reflection when a learner consciously looks at his or her prior beliefs and revises old assumptions in favor of new. Critical self-reflection, however, is difficult to achieve in an 8-hour safety training session, particularly if the materials and information presented are out of date, irrelevant, or boring. Stories can provide shortcuts to self-reflection and thus transformational learning by making boring material interesting and by

> [O]ne of the theories for why stories are remembered so well is that you are using your 'whole brain' to take in information.... Stories allow a person to feel and see the information as well as factually understand it... [B]ecause you 'hear' the information factually, visually, and emotionally, it is more likely to be imprinted on your brain in a way that it sticks with you longer with very little effort on your part. (1993, pp. 4-5)

MacDonald reinforces this idea with a lyrical story of her own. " 'I have heard,' said the philosopher, 'that the head does not hear anything until the heart has listened, and what the heart knows today the head will understand tomorrow' " (1993, p. 43).

Miners are storytellers. One need only spend time with them to observe that they interact with each other through the telling of stories. Such stories may be about close calls they have had, about other master miners they have known and worked with (and in many cases, learned from), about someone they knew who made an error in judgment and paid dearly for it, or about things they have seen and experienced as they have gone through their careers. The role of miners' stories is complex and includes the sharing and strengthening of their occupational culture as well as the bonding that must exist to survive in a dangerous environment.

A primary role of storytelling, however, is the education of inexperienced miners. Experienced miners see these people

as a potential hazard to everyone in the mine if the way they make decisions and carry out their work isn't in alignment with culturally acceptable practices. Experienced miners understand that one thoughtless or dangerous act can put ev-

eryone in peril. It is in their best interest to teach inexperienced workers how to do the job correctly. Their own lives may depend on it. Billett explains it this way: "Developing learners' conceptual understanding of why things are done a certain way and what would happen if they were not, is a key role" (1994, p. 13).

Cole has done extensive research into the role of storytelling and its relationship to training, particularly in the mining industry. In his work, he has investigated the use of narrative-based simulations to teach particular skills or ideas. He discusses the concept of "narrative thinking" as the process of—

translation of one's own and others' experiences into stories that integrate facts, perceptions, emotions, intentions, actions, and consequences into coherent meaning. Storytelling is not the only successful cognitive process for organizing perception, thought, memory and action, but...it is more effective than any other. (1997, p. 331)

As noted earlier, federal law mandates that miners receive safety training (CFR 30 46.4(3). It is, in the opinion of the lawmakers and regulators, critical that they receive what Bruner (1990) would call "socially relevant information." Turning the facts and statistics from socially relevant (defined as what the experts think you should know) into personally relevant information has long been the challenge of trainers, however. As Cole points out, "many learners who receive...this formally codified and socially relevant knowledge tend to find both the content and the instruction to be burdensome, dull, and boring" (1997, p. 334). Stories turn impersonal statistics into faces—people

just like the listeners—who may have suffered injury or death on the job. Because of the shared sense of danger and camaraderie felt in the culture of mining, it is not difficult for learners to transfer themselves into the story and think about how they would have reacted or what they would have done. This is immensely powerful when teaching the "why should I care?" about safety.

Miller, Oaks, and Akmal provide very pragmatic guidance for the design and delivery of training materials useful to the mining industry. Using current adult learning theories, characteristics of the mining culture, and information provided by mine safety trainers, they list the following criteria as critical to effective training.

- Materials and activities should focus on visual and hands-on learning.
- Training should be grounded in authentic events and situations.
- Materials need to be interesting and motivating.

- Materials should be applicable to both groups and individuals.
- Materials and activities should be consistent with the interests and characteristics of learners.
- Activities should be practical, immediately useful, and focused on authentic training.
- Effective training combines similar concepts rather than presenting small unrelated topics.
- Training materials need to be cost effective.
- Training should be realistic and practiced in real environments.
- Materials and activities should be easy to use.
- Materials and activities should be flexible for a variety of settings and learners. (1998, pp. 8-9)

These criteria are consistent with the theoretical models already presented and serve to emphasize the practical nature of safety trainers in the industry. Their primary responsibility is to provide the information and knowledge necessary to assure that both experienced and inexperienced miners go home safely at the end of every shift.

Zemke (2002) was correct in stating that, in order for anyone to learn new information or skills, they first must pay attention and then remember what they are taught. In the end, trainees must make the decision to both learn and use the information presented because they recognize its validity and its value to their success in their work, not because it is the organization's policy that they do so.

The challenge to the new NIOSH research project was clear. Safety trainers and specialists admitted their need for new materials to teach specific mine safety topics, but for these materials and the trainers that presented them to be effective, a new way of providing information had to be found. Two major forces already existed in the mining industry that could be drawn upon in the creation of new training materials: The existence of a powerful occupational culture that valued and relied upon a strong master-apprenticeship training model and an oral tradition of storytelling handed down over centuries. These two forces would become the foundation for the theoretical frameworks used to develop truly effective safety training for miners.

RESEARCH APPROACH

By Elaine T. Cullen

The initial request for effective safety training materials came to NIOSH through the stakeholder meetings held at numerous locations throughout the West. At these meetings, mining professionals were asked to participate in facilitated information-gathering sessions to provide data on critical research needs that NIOSH could help them meet. One such need was for up-to-date, interesting training materials, and late in 1998, NIOSH funded a small-scale pilot project to investigate what could be done. Before starting the development phase of the project, additional meetings were held with small groups of mine safety trainers to determine what training topics were most important and what media were most commonly used.

The principal investigator made the decision at this time to focus the project on underground hard-rock problems. SRL's sister laboratory in the East, the Pittsburgh Research Laboratory (PRL), had a proven track record of creating training materials for coal miners, and with a small budget, it was obvious that it was necessary to limit the parameters of the project in order to be successful. In time, the scope of the project was widened to include surface and aggregate operations, The development of coal mine training materials was continued by researchers at PRL. As it quickly became obvious that most mine sites did not have access to computer laboratories, a second decision was made that computers were not to be considered as a medium for providing the new training materials.

The issue of "handling explosives" was at the top of the short list of prioritized training topics. In-depth interviews with safety specialists interested in this topic determined that many types of explosives were in use in underground mines, as well as a variety of specific hazards associated with working near explosives. We decided to focus on general safety for all miners rather than specific task training for blasters. MSHA regulations particular to handling different types of explosives were taken as the starting point, and the MSHA Accident and Injury database, an excellent source of statistics on mining-related injuries (accessible through its Website at www.msha.gov), provided information on all accidents directly attributable to explosives in an underground environment.

Conversations with explosives experts identified individuals who might have stories related to explosives accidents to tell. Armed with these resources, a storyline was developed that included the more common problems associated with handling explosives, and several underground mines were contacted to arrange shoot sites for the video.

Process

The process of developing the training videos themselves evolved along with the project. SRL does not have the in-house capability to produce professional-quality digital video, so after a competitive bidding process, an outside contractor, the local AT&T[4] production studio (now owned by ComCast) was selected to do this work. The professional crew, made up of a videographer and a production manager, provided the technical expertise, professional-quality videograhic equipment to gather the footage, and the high-end hardware and software to edit it into a concise, interesting training piece. It was necessary to train the members of the crew in all general and specific hazards of mining, and to overcome the logistical challenges faced by taping in an environment that could range from below 0 °F on the surface to over 100 °F underground. Humidity, groundwater, dust, and diesel fumes also posed problems for the film crew and their sensitive equipment.

The value of the experience gained and the specific knowledge learned by both the professional film crew and by SRL staff as the project progressed made it practical to use the same crew for all the videos. Real miners were employed in all the videos rather than professional actors, researchers, or regulators. These people were generally uncomfortable in front of the cameras, but the crew developed an excellent rapport with the miners, helping and encouraging them throughout. Without that connection, it is doubtful the results would have been satisfactory.

Many hard-rock miners work under a "gypo," or contract, system. This means that while the miners are

---

[4]The mention of specific products, manufacturers, and companies does not constitute endorsement by the National Institute for Occupational Safety and Health.

paid an hourly wage based on experience, expertise, and work assignment, they can also earn substantial production bonuses. Because this system puts pressure on miners to work hard and fast to maximize their bonuses, many people in the mining industry doubted that miners would be willing to take time to "be in the movies." Any time they spent working with the film production crew meant lost wages. There was also a very real concern that the miners would not be willing to cooperate with a government agency.

Both of these fears proved groundless. The miners were generally delighted to be asked to participate. They are proud people and eager to talk about what they do. If anything, a very lively competition developed at the film sites as miners vied with each other to be included in the videos. In an occupational culture that values expertise and the status it provides, being chosen as an acclaimed mentor and "movie star" guaranteed bragging rights.

When shooting a training video that stars nonprofessional actors, especially those who may never have been taped before, it is important to be, above all else, patient. Miners were not given scripts to memorize. (Early attempts at using a more formal script proved that it would be both frustrating and unproductive.) They were only told what things they needed to talk about and then were allowed to do so in their own words and in their own way. If something was not covered, we merely continued to shoot as they talked about that issue and then edited the segment to make sure all the important topics were covered. We worked very hard to maintain a fun, friendly, laid-back environment and to assure the miners at all times that they were doing a great job. In some cases, we provided them a new hire to talk

with that helped the miners organize their thinking and their teaching. Most of the older miners we worked with had trained new people, and when we asked them to pretend they had a new young partner, they had no trouble instructing him, easily falling into the roles of mentor and teacher.

Having the right people to act as master-miners or young new miners is critical to the development of effective safety training, and the safety directors and managers at the cooperating mines did a wonderful job of identifying and screening potential miner-actors. They were well aware of which people at their sites did the best job of performing different tasks, as well as who had a good sense of humor or who would be willing to participate.

At no time did we show up unannounced in a stope or at a working face and expect people to drop everything to work with us. The miners were always warned that we were coming, and they always had the option of whether to be part of the filming or not. Such a prearrangement had the dual benefit of assuring that when we arrived, the miners would be ready to film, which would minimize their own downtime and maximize our productivity underground. It also gave the miners time to think about how they would do things, what they would talk about, what equipment or props they needed to have on hand, and, in many cases, suggestions about other topics or scenes that should be included that we might not have thought about. They were the masters, and we followed their advice whenever it was possible to do so. If we had been tied to a strict storyboard, with no room for improvisation or additions, this would have been quite frustrating, but because we followed a fairly loose storyline, the videos tended to grow and become as we progressed.

Products

Handling Explosives in Underground Mines **(1999)**

The first video produced, *Handling Explosives in Underground Mines* (Cullen, 1999) (figure 1), was approximately 15 minutes long. When released, it was very well received by the industry. The miners, we were told, really liked watching and hearing from people who looked like themselves. They also had no trouble associating with and understanding the stories of the explosives disasters described.

After the video's release, the advisory group of safety and training specialists reconvened and developed a further list of training materials that they believed were needed by the industry.

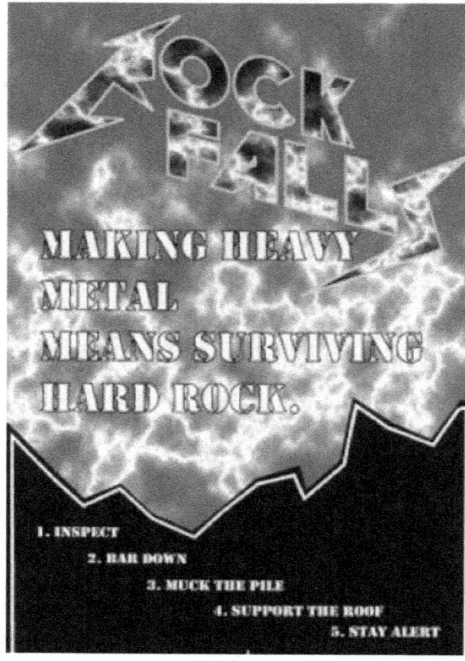

Figure 2.—*Rock Falls: Preventing Rock Falls in Underground Noncoal Mines* video poster.

Rock Falls: Preventing Rock Fall Injuries in Underground Non-Coal Mines **(1999)**

The only video produced at SRL that was not an actual part of the initial research project was *Rock Falls: Preventing Rock Fall Injuries in Underground Non-Coal Mines* (Miller, 1999) (figure 2). This 20-minute video was produced under a separate research project (thus separate funding) in which roof hazard recognition and effective scaling techniques were being investigated. When safety trainers asked the project researchers to put together a training video to show what they had learned, the same production crew was employed. Not only was this video well-received by the mining industry, but it also won NIOSH's Alice Hamilton Award for Excellence in Educational Materials for 2000.

Figure 1.—*Handling Explosives in Underground Mines* video poster.

Figure 3.—*Miner Mike Saves the Day* video poster.

Miner Mike Saves the Day--or-- Ground Support: It's Important (2000)

In *Miner Mike Saves the Day* (Cullen, 2000) (figure 3), a story was created that featured two lazy, young miners who decide that leaving out vital roof supports would not be noticed by anyone and would save them from having to work too hard. An older, wiser miner observes this behavior and teaches them how roof supports work, why they need to be installed as planned, and what happens when they are not. He then takes them around the mine to meet other experts who explain different types of supports, how they should be installed properly and how to tell if they are not, and what to do if there is a problem. The Miner Mike video starred 14 separate miners working in five different mines. This video also won an Alice Hamilton Award for Excellence in Educational Materials in 2001.

Hazards in Motion (2001)

Hazards in Motion (Cullen, 2001a) (figures 4 and 5) furthers the use of storytelling by creating not only a brash young miner, Ben, who refuses to pay attention during his new-miner training, but also an "angel of safety." This "angel" acts as a mentor, conscience, and protector of young Ben as he learns that his behavior puts everyone in danger, particularly himself. In this video, Ben wanders around the mine, clueless but cocky. He encounters many types of mobile equipment (mobile equipment is one of the major contributors

Figure 4.—Filming of the *Hazards in Motion* video.

to injuries in underground environments), as well as expert miners who teach him about proper safety checks, equipment operating procedures, and accepted behavioral norms. Under the safety angel's watchful eye, Ben learns much about mobile equipment

Figure 5.—*Hazards in Motion* video poster.

Hidden Scars (2001)

During the filming of *You Are My Sunshine* (see below), many, if not most, of the miners interviewed shared stories about their careers in the mines. Some of these stories were about near-misses they had experienced, the miners who had trained them as new hands, or the friends and co-workers lost over the years to mining accidents. One of the most poignant stories was told by Don Capparelli. He described a rock burst in 1994 that buried him alive for 3 hours and killed his long-time partner and best friend, Jimmy Finlay.[5] Don's story was captured in its entirety and released as *Hidden Scars* (Cullen, 2001b) (figure 6). In it, Don talks about what it is like not being able to move or even breathe and to feel his partner struggle beneath him and eventually die. It's a stark reminder of the hidden cost of industrial accidents—the physical and psychological scars that are carried by the victims forever, as well as the impact such tragedies have on colleagues and co-workers.

and finally realizes that he, himself, is the major mobile hazard underground.

This video makes use of several important constructs, including the role of the master-mentor and the transitional character who gains knowledge and wisdom as a result of near-miss errors in judgment. It also uses storytelling and humor to break down barriers, encourage learning, and increase the attention span of viewers. *Hazards in Motion* won a national award for outstanding achievement from the Centers for Disease Control and Prevention's Communicators Roundtable in the Electronic Media category in 2002.

Figure 6.—*Hidden Scars* video poster.

---

[5]A report on this rock burst is available from NIOSH (Whyatt, Williams, & White, 2000).

Review

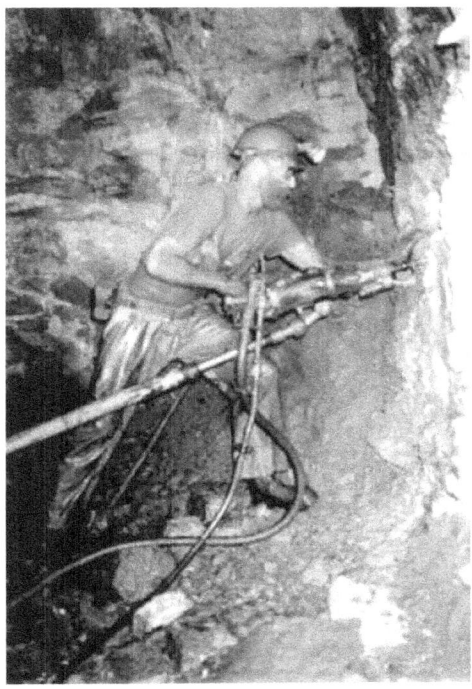

As each video neared completion, it was put through a rigorous technical review process that included showing the draft version to technical and safety mining experts as well as to researchers with specific expertise in the topic of the video. Both written and verbal comments were gathered on how well the video provided information on the subject in question, whether the information was accurate, whether the information was complete, what other subtopics should have been included, and whether or not the video was interesting and generally appealing. (Appendix A shows a sample technical review questionnaire.) Focus-group-type meetings were held also, but always with subject matter experts as the primary source of the information gathered. These comments were used to make adjustments to the videos before they were submitted to the Office of the Director of NIOSH in Washington, DC, for approval. Accompanying materials to be included with the video were also subjected to a technical review.

When the Washington office staff had approved the video for release, mine safety trainers across the country were notified through an electronic list serve, by notices posted on the NIOSH Website, or through distribution of a two-page *Technology News.* Information was also made available to the safety community through related association newsletters, conference exhibits, and presentations and talks given at various meetings and conferences.

Copies of the videos are provided free of charge to safety trainers who request them. In order to build and maintain an accurate customer database, however, SRL controls the distribution of the videos. This database allowed us to obtain feedback on how the videos were being used and whether they met the training needs of our safety training customers, as well as to collect information for future training topics.

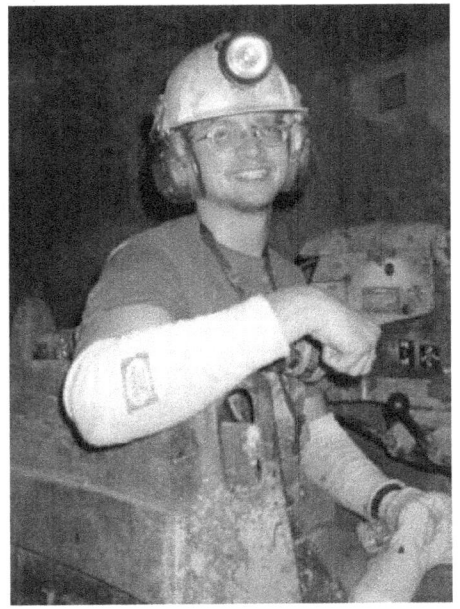

EVALUATION

By Albert H. Fein

Training evaluation can mean many things depending on who is doing the evaluation and what they want to find out. Mallett and Reinke (2002) note that evaluations can pertain to the instructor, the class, the materials, the classroom, or just about any other subject about which those who authorized the training want to know. Evaluations may involve informal conversations, focus groups, or highly structured surveys. The controlling factors are the needs of the interested parties and the resources available to carry out the evaluation.

Kirkpatrick (2001) offers a four-level evaluation scheme in which data-gathering progresses from the easiest and most informal mode to the most difficult and resource-intensive. In this scheme, the trainees are evaluated for (1) reaction or perceptions about the training, (2) knowledge or skills that were improved as a result of the training, (3) changes in behavior or adoption of new knowledge or skills, and (4) overall impact on the organization. While gathering perceptions from trainees or even measuring what they have learned as a result of the training is relatively simple and quick, adequately assessing how behaviors have changed over time or how an organization has changed as a result of training takes a long time and requires a good deal of resources. (In the case of mining, this would generally translate into a change in accident rates in a specific area for which the miners were trained.) To truly measure the impact of a specific training class or product, Kirkpatrick suggests that measuring the performance of trained workers against the performance of a control group of untrained workers would be optimal. Obviously, in a

mining environment where it is legally mandated that all workers be trained, it is impractical and likely impossible to designate an untrained control group for the sole purpose of testing the effectiveness of training materials. The ethical problem of sending untrained workers into a dangerous environment would preclude any evaluation measure that suggested it.

A further complication in adequately evaluating the effectiveness of individual training products arises when the demographics of the worker population is considered. While new miners are beginning to enter the industry, for the most part, miners in the United States are "mature" in that their average age is around 50. These are not inexperienced workers, and to assume that viewing the NIOSH videos on specific required safety and health topics is their first exposure to that information would be a serious error. The videos are used for this worker population as part of their refresher training, which could best be described as reminder training. This is not new information to them, but is merely presented in a new, more interesting fashion. The goal of the videos in this environment is to remind workers of the dangers and of their own role in avoiding them.

In spite of these challenges, Mallett and Reinke (2002) offer several options for gathering data about the effectiveness of training. Among these are questionnaires, interviews, group discussions, pretest/post-test surveys, and others. While it may be argued that some methods provide more "truth" than others, all can add to the body of evaluation data. Kirkpatrick states, "Something beats nothing, and I encourage trainers to at least do some evaluation of behavior, even if it isn't elaborate or scientific" (2001, p. 128).

In April 2001, NIOSH funded an independent research team from Gonzaga University, Drs. Fein and Isaacson (2001), to evaluate the five videos (*Handling Explosives in Modern Mines, Preventing Rock Fall Injuries in Underground Non-Coal Mines, Miner Mike Saves the Day–or–Ground Support...It's Important, Hazards in Motion,* and *Hidden Scars*) that had been or were about to be released. The charge to the evaluators was to determine whether or not the videos were effective as teaching tools.

The first three videos had been out for 2 or 3 years by the time the evaluation began. Other than initial technical reviews to fine-tune the videos before their release, no formal in-house evaluations had been done. Obviously, exclusive use of a pre-test/post-test format was impossible because many of the miners in the target audience had already viewed them, and that would have skewed any data gathered.

For these three training videos, then, other methods were utilized, including phone interviews with trainers, e-mail requests for feedback from trainers, and post-tests for trainees. Obtaining feedback from miners and safety trainers about the content and impact of the videos was the primary goal.

Pre-tests to be used in subsequent new miner training were still developed for these three videos, however. These workers would not have seen the videos previously, so while it was too late to gather pre-test information from trained miners, valid data could still be gathered from new trainees using a pre-test/post-test model.

Hazards in Motion and *Hidden Scars* were released after the evaluation contract was awarded. Originally, both videos were to be released in early June of 2001, but on the day of the anticipated "world premier," one of the miners (along with his new partner) who had participated in the *Hazards in Motion* video was killed in a rock burst similar to the one that Don Capparelli describes in *Hidden Scars*. Release of both videos was therefore delayed until August of 2001, and a statement in memory of the miner who lost his life, as well as a tribute to all miners who had died in the mines, was added to *Hazards in Motion.*

Pre- and post-test questionnaires were developed for both videos and packaged with the initial distribution of the videos to mine safety professionals. The intent was that the trainer would distribute the questionnaires to the miners involved in the annual refresher training, as well as to any new hires undergoing their initial safety training. A questionnaire was also created to obtain information from the trainers themselves about their perceptions of the effectiveness and usefulness of the video being shown. A cover letter accompanied each video asking trainers to administer the survey to their students, fill out their own evaluations, and send all the completed evaluations back to SRL. If trainers chose to add their own comments about the videos, these were included in the phone interview data gathered by the evaluators.

It is important to note that participation in the evaluation process was entirely voluntary. Miners were not required to take either test and were not questioned if they opted not to participate. Similarly, trainers were not required to respond or to use the assessment tools if they chose not to, and no record was kept of which ones did and which ones did not participate.

Multiple-choice or true-false questions were used for evaluating videos 1 through 4. An objective test format was chosen for ease of correction, and scores for both pre- and post-tests were based on the percentage of correct answers (the number of correct responses divided by the number of possible responses). (See Appendix B for sample pre-tests and post-tests.) Test items were developed by the evaluation team based on the content of the narration of each film. Data gathered from the surveys showed that generally, post-test scores were higher than pre-test scores and that there was a substantial difference in learning improvement between miners identified as experienced (over 1 year of mining experience) and those who were categorized as inexperienced (less than 1 year). As might be expected, inexperienced miners generally showed more improvement in knowledge as a result of watching the videos than did experienced miners.

There were, however, two major weaknesses in the design of the numeric evaluation method for these four videos.

The first was that pre-test questions were mostly true-false or multiple choice. Therefore, it was relatively easy to guess correctly just using common sense. In fact, a control group of nonminers (college students) taking these tests scored as well or better than many of the miners, both experienced and inexperienced. (One explanation for the students' high scores on the tests may be that they were more comfortable with taking tests in general than the miners were.) The second weakness in the design was that because participation was voluntary and the videos had already been used by many safety trainers, the number of tests turned in was too low to be statistically sound.

An objective test format was not appropriate for *Hidden Scars*. The pre-test and post-test format used for this video consisted of open-ended questions that had no "right" answers (see Appendix C). These tests were evaluated using qualitative data analysis methods. Responses were analyzed by looking for patterns and themes that included whether viewers were engaged in the story and how they perceived the lessons it taught.

Again, a control group of college-age nonminers was invited to view *Hazards in Motion* and *Hidden Scars* and to participate in the pre- and post-tests. These people had little experience with mining operations or safety issues and provided a control group that was a good match for the minimal knowledge base of new miners. Because the training videos were intended for use by both new and experienced miners, it was important to differentiate the two groups and to gather

Table 1.— Mean improvement score among experienced and inexperienced miners

Title	Experienced miners, %	Inexperienced miners, %
Explosives Underground	11.30	12.60
Rock Falls	0.40	14.60
Miner Mike Saves the Day	6.10	9.40
Hazards in Motion	11.60	9.60

data on both. A sample of responses for *Hidden Scars* is given below.

Experienced miners:
- I found this movie to be emotional and honest. It makes a person take a look at the small things most people take for granted as well as showing how fragile life really is.
- It was really good. It really made me think about the dangers of mining. It made me think about what it would be like to be buried and lose a partner and how tough and hard that could be.
- I may not be the one hurt or killed but may have to live the rest of my life with the memory of another person's inj

Inexperienced miners:
- It's a scary thought and fact that this does happen. That's why you must be prepared and aware.
- I thought it was a good reality check for what really goes on in mines. It was a very touching video that makes you realize the importance of safety.
- Through no fault of their own, one person literally lost his life and another lost the type of life he had. The survivor will have to deal with that accident for the rest of his life... emotional scars are sometimes more destructive than physical ones. We all need to be aware that things can happen and

Characteristics of adult learners and of miners in particular were taken into account during the production of these safety videos, so the evaluation assessment attempted to measure miners' attitudes regarding the videos in addition to evaluating their effectiveness in increasing knowledge about mine safety. To this end, each post-test contained three statements to which the test taker could respond on a five-point Likert scale.

- [Name of video] taught me something I did not know.
- [Name of video] "talked down" to me.
- [Name of video] was enjoyable to watch. (Fein and Isaacson, 2001, p. 5)

A space for comments was also provided. These statements allowed the test takers to offer their own assessments about the worthiness of the content, whether the tone of the video reflected the characteristics of adult learners and miners, and whether they found the video engaging.

Interviews of Mining Safety Trainers and Safety Experts

Phone interviews were conducted with a representative sample of the 554 individuals who had requested copies of one or more of the films at the time the study began. The participants for phone interviews were selected by the interviewers using a table of random numbers. If the individual selected by this procedure worked at a mine outside the United States or no e-mail address or phone number could be found, the next name on the list was selected. Five of the technical experts and safety leaders in mining who had been consulted when the videos were developed were also interviewed by phone.

Phone interviews were conducted between August and November 2001. Of the 554 names, 70 (12.6%) were selected for phone interviews. The length of time of interviews ranged from 5 to 25 minutes and averaged 10 minutes. The interview questions were open-ended. Participants were asked which of the five videos they had seen and/or used in training. If the video had been used in training, participants were asked whether it had been shown to new and/or experienced miners. Participants were then asked to give their general impression of the individual videos or all the videos taken together. Follow-up questions about the quality or effectiveness of the video for training and how the audience responded to the videos were also asked. Interviewers sought for specificity without leading the participant. For example, if participants made a generally positive comment, such as "Good movie," the interviewer might follow up with "Say more about that" or "What specifically made it good?" Interviewers took handwritten notes during interviews and transcribed them immediately afterward

into electronic Word documents.

Thirty-nine of the 70 people contacted agreed to be interviewed. Of the 31 individuals who were contacted but not interviewed, about a dozen declined because they had requested mining safety video(s) but had never received them, two declined because they worked for NIOSH, and the rest never responded to the messages left by the interviewers. Except for one individual, whose phone number was incorrect, all 70 potential interviewees were either interviewed or received at least one message requesting an interview. All sources of evaluative data were triangulated to offer the most complete picture of the efficacy of each video.

Of the 39 completed phone interviews, four (10.2%) were with female participants and 35 (89.8%) were with males. This finding matches Miller's (1998) description of the characteristics of miners as predominantly male.

Most of those interviewed were mining safety trainers or individuals who were responsible for mining safety training but who held other titles (mine

36

be due to the types of mines that would be interested in underground hard rock mining safety videos, although some of the participants interviewed for this evaluation did work in above-ground mines or at coal mines.

In addition to the phone contacts, e-mail requests for feedback were sent to approximately 60 individuals. About half the e-mails came back as undeliverable, and of those that were delivered, only a portion generated responses. For those who did respond, the e-mails were printed and added to the data set.

supervisor, director of public outreach, safety specialist, foreman, manager, supervisor of transportation, human resources director, mine inspector, underground safety mining engineer, professor, and geologist). One participant was the owner of a gold mine that had been in his family for three generations and did not consider himself to be a full-time professional miner. However, the majority of individuals interviewed worked for mines. Participants from outside the United States were not included in the evaluation.

Nineteen different states are represented in the phone interview data. Thirty-three percent of the interviewees were located in either Idaho or Nevada, and 23% were located in Arizona, Colorado, Washington, or Utah. States where only one phone contact was made included California, Georgia, Kansas, Louisiana, Maryland, Missouri, Montana, New Mexico, Pennsylvania, Tennessee, Texas, Virginia, and Wyoming. Therefore, although mines in both the eastern and western United States were represented in the phone interview sample, over 80% were located west of the Mississippi River. This result may

General Overview of Evaluation Results

Five video training films were included in the initial evaluation study—*Explosives Underground, Rock Falls: Preventing Rock Fall Injuries in Underground Mines, Miner Mike Saves the Day-or-Ground Support...It's Important, Hazards in Motion,* and *Hidden Scars.* Most of the participants had seen more than one of the videos, and many reported having seen all five.

Participants who had seen more than one of the videos commonly offered their opinions about all the videos they had seen rather than speaking about one particular title. Sometimes this was because they had viewed the videos months prior to the interview, and they were unable to recall details about each title. (Since annual refresher training is generally held once a year, it was possible that nearly a year had elapsed between the time the trainer had watched the video and the time when he or she was contacted by the evaluation team.)

Some participants remarked that the videos were of a similar quality and that it was easier for them to comment upon them collectively. While several individuals were very articulate and offered detailed analyses of the videos, others found it difficult to provide reasons for their views when asked to elaborate on their comments.

As the evaluation process proceeded, several themes emerged from the written comments and interviews. What follows is a compilation of the major themes expressed without reference to specific titles. For confidentiality purposes, none of the safety experts or miners interviewed by phone or in person will be identified by name or location. No names or addresses were collected on the forms mailed to trainers soliciting written responses. Participants were asked only to provide their years of experience in the industry, so that evaluators could separate new miners from those who had over 1 year of mining experience. The purpose was to determine if a difference could be detected between the two groups with regard to how they related to and learned from the videos.

Quality

A strong theme that emerged from these general assessments of the videos was their high quality. One participant noted that he had produced his own safety films and appreciated how well done these videos were. He said they had good story lines and provided good information. Another individual, who had seen all the films and used one in his training program, said he would use others. He stated—

> Excellent films. On a scale of one to five, these are 10 stars. The use of real miners who tell their own story or explain how to do things was very effective. These films serve their purpose well and are well done. Miners who view them enjoy and understand the films.

He added that other films he had used had cheap production values, were out of date, or were very expensive to purchase. Another participant stated, "These were among the best training films I've ever used. Certainly the best training films in 30 years because they are by miners, in mines, and very relevant to their needs." Another commented, "It is very hard to find good quality, up-to-date videos to train with and these were perfect." One participant expressed gratitude for the videos and commented that new videos were a welcome change. He said, "Audiences appreciate that the videos are up to date. They just get sick of same old videos."

Credibility

One of the comments repeated almost universally throughout the study related to the credibility of the videos. According to participants, the videos were credible because they were filmed underground in real mines with real miners as actors and presented realistic situations to which miners could relate. Comments included—

- Real-life story made them effective. Touches home. The audience never fell asleep. Videos kept them interested the whole time.

- They were realistic. The audience loved that they were real miners.

- Miners respond to and relate to the films because they are down to earth and realistic. Miners as actors added credibility.

- Use of real miners—not paid actors—and real mines—underground—are key factors.

- Real guys. Real mines. Real situations.

- They are not studio films. They are filmed underground in real settings.

- I liked the use of miners to tell stories. Nice approach. Liked the miner-to-miner tone. Gets the point across.

These comments would seem to corroborate the research done by Zemke (2000) in which he claims that adults are much more likely to pay attention to and to learn by watching others if those others are similar to themselves. From the comments gathered by the evaluation team, the miners enjoyed watching "actors" who were real miners and appreciated the fact that the videos were shot in real mines and showed situations that could occur in those mines.

Another key factor appeared to be that the language spoken in the videos was that commonly used by real miners. All of the actor-mentors told their stories or instructed the younger miners in language they use every day, not in language that was scripted by outsiders. This provided an authenticity to the videos that would not have been possible if more technical language had been used or if the actors were nonminers. These comments also proved the validity of allowing miners to talk about their subjects in their own words rather than following a scripted text.

Content

Many comments praised the videos for their content. Participants in the evaluation appreciated that a lot of information was presented in a fairly short time and that mining issues were well-depicted. One participant praised "the specifics and up-to-dateness of the films." Another appreciated how the videos "demonstrate right and wrong practices." Another participant stated that the videos "address important safety issues. The content is appropriate to the work [miners] do. They are not generic safety films. That is important to the miners."

Effectiveness of Videos as an Educational Tool

Another strong theme was the effectiveness of the videos as educational vehicles. Many participants felt they could be used successfully with both new and experienced miners or even with other types of audiences. One participant stated, "Excellent refreshers for experienced folks and for new miner indoctrination. Great for introducing people with no underground experience to that work setting. Very effective for preparing new miners before they are taken underground." One interviewee reported that he uses the videos extensively in training with new and experienced miners and that after viewing the films, miners ask questions and "they remember details." Many commented that the safety messages came through, such as the need to use safety gear. One participant stated, "The videos made a sometimes difficult topic (safety) entertaining while communicating important information."

A mining professional, who was one of the stakeholders who participated as a technical advisor in the preproduction stages, felt that the films met the needs expressed by the stakeholders during the stakeholder meetings. He felt that more such films were needed and that "training and education are the best tools to prevent injuries and accidents."

Quite often the participant who viewed or used the video did not work in an underground mine, but nevertheless found the videos to be of value. One stated, "Even though the video shows miners using jacklegs—we use different equipment in this mine—it still hits home."

Engagement

Participants generally found the videos to be engaging due to their relevance, appropriate length, use of humor, and ease of understanding. The stories were "told from the employee point of view." Other comments that reflected this theme include—

- They were short, to the point and interesting.

- I appreciated the use of humor.

- Very effective, to the point; not repetitious or boring. They reinforce important ideas.

- Miners really liked the films. Not too long.

- We have 8 hours of mandatory training. The miners usually fall asleep. They don't with these films. Good mix of humor and serious. Keep making these.

- The films do not contain a lot of charts and diagrams, yet they speak about important issues in simple terms—miner to miner.

- The comedic tone is almost hokey, yet it keeps your interest and allows miners to laugh at themselves while still pointing out how [wrong] decisions can put you at risk.

The researchers who produced the videos made it a primary goal to honor the work and life experiences of the miners who would be viewing them and to show respect for the expertise these people had gained. One participant addressed this aspect of the training videos by saying, "The audience didn't feel talked down to."

Value to Other Audiences

Not all the trainers and audiences who viewed the videos worked in underground mines. Many users represented surface or preparation plant operations or even nonmining industries. The videos have proven to be of interest to these audiences and in fact have found their way into many training rooms that have little, if anything, to do with mining. One participant reported that his work often called for providing historical documentation of abandoned mines. He said that he would share films with his peers. Many participants were eager to see other videos produced: "Keep up the good work." "Don't change what they've got." "Just keep making more." "They are on to something unique and need to keep it up."

YOU ARE MY SUNSHINE

By Elaine T. Cullen

In 2001, work began on a video with an entirely different focus. The advisory group had expressed a need for materials that could be used to train mine rescue teams. Knowing that the Sunshine Mine, located east of Kellogg, ID, had been the site of a disastrous fire in 1972, the principal investigator decided to use the Sunshine as a backdrop for a mine rescue video. Don Capparelli, who played the angel of safety in the video *Hazards in Motion*, was a supervisor at the Sunshine Mine in 2001 and was working at the mine when the fire broke out in 1972. He had also been a member of the rescue and recovery crew during that time, knew everyone still working at the mine who had been employed there in May 1972,[6] and was both able and willing to act as an intermediary for the project.

Don obtained support for the project from Sunshine management and arranged interviews with 27 people. These participants fell into four main categories: (1) survivors of the fire who had escaped the mine, (2) rescue and recovery workers who had searched for survivors, worked to bring the fire under control, restored critical systems to the mine so that recovery efforts could continue, or brought out the bodies of 91 of their friends and co-workers, (3) the two men (Tom Wilkerson and Ron Flory) who had survived the fire and were rescued after being trapped underground for 8 days, and (4) family and community members who waited at the surface for word of their loved ones.

Figure 7.—*You Are My Sunshine* video poster.

You Are My Sunshine (Cullen, 2002a) (figure 7) incorporates the many stories told by the interviewees into a case study of the fire itself. It discusses what happened, what went wrong, and most importantly, what lessons were learned. In many cases, the stories told by the Sunshine survivors and their friends and families had never been voiced before. The culture of hard-rock mining prohibited, to some degree, their sharing these stories with wives or loved ones, and although the mine and its subsystems (ground control plan, ventilation system, evacuation plans, etc.) had been extensively studied after the fire by state and federal agencies, for the most part no one had ever asked the miners themselves about their experiences. (A few individuals had been asked to testify at Congressional hearings or

---

[6]This fire was the catalyst for passage of the Mine Safety and Health Act of 1977—known in the mining industry as "the Act"—that brought metal and nonmetal mining under the same rigorous health, safety, and training requirements that governed coal mining.

during the trials that followed the fire, but most of the men interviewed for the Sunshine video were not in this group.)

Wilkerson and Flory had been interviewed extensively by journalists as a result of their "miraculous" survival and rescue. Because of their perception that the news media were often overly aggressive and intrusive when covering the Sunshine story, they were apprehensive at first. By the time most of their co-workers had been through their own interviews and were able to reassure Wilkerson and Flory that the process was not invasive, they agreed to participate.

The Sunshine Mining Company was in the last stages of bankruptcy at the time *You Are My Sunshine* was being filmed. It was difficult, if not impossible, to get information from corporate offices (headquartered in Boise, ID, and in Texas), but local management couldn't have been more cooperative. Free access was given to the miners and the mine, and a dedicated guide and assistant (Don Capparelli) was provided to help with anything we needed to do.

It is worth noting that the bankruptcy of the company and imminent closure of the mine may have played a role in the willingness of the miners to finally talk about their experiences during the fire. The Silver Valley is a geographically and, to some degree, socially isolated place. Its citizens can be suspicious of outsiders, and they have no great love for "gommint people" who are perceived by them as trying to control their lives. In addition, there were numerous "legends" that had grown up around the fire, most of which were far from factual, but tended to be quite negative and hurtful.

When the Sunshine miners were asked why they agreed to participate in the filming of this video, many stated that it was time to tell the story and that

Figure 8.—NIOSH conducting interviews at the Sunshine Mine.

by sharing their experiences with others in the mining industry, it was their hope that no one else would ever have to go through a similar experience. They feared that if the mine were closed, their last chance to tell their stories would be lost. Many had seen the safety training videos SRL had produced and enjoyed them very much. They believed that (1) we understood mining, (2) we wouldn't make them look stupid, and (3) unlike members of the news media who had descended on them at the time, we would tell the truth about the fire.

Interviews (figure 8) were conducted primarily at three sites: a little-used battery barn on the 2700 level of the mine just off the Jewel shaft station (which is the main entrance to the mine), the safety training room on the surface, and the back room of Sweets Tavern, a favorite local bar. The separate locations assured that everyone could be interviewed, whether underground workers, surface workers, or retired workers and community members.

The same format and questions were used for each group when appropriate, although the interviews themselves tended to be flexible in order to capture the range of experiences. In all cases, the interviews were private. Only the film crew, the interviewer, and the interviewee were present. Not only did this reduce the anxiety of the miners as they sat in front of the cameras, it also assured that they did not "play to their co-workers" when telling their stories and made it possible to triangulate the data to some degree.

The miners were asked to talk about what they were doing when the fire broke out, what conditions were like underground during the fire, what actions people took when they realized there was a serious problem, and how they escaped. For those not working underground, information was gathered on what their role was in the rescue and recovery, what conditions were like on the surface as the community came to realize the extent of the disaster, what was included in the rescue effort, and what the long-term impact of the fire was on the mine and the community. The two men found alive after 8 days were asked to provide a detailed description of their experiences.

None of the miners knew what others had said in their interviews, and although it is likely that there was some talk and information-sharing as the men waited for their turn outside of the interview areas, most miners did not see the finished product until it was premiered nearly 18 months later. (A representative group of participants, managers, and safety professionals was asked, however, to participate as technical reviewers as the video began to take shape. Comments and suggestions from this group were incorporated into the final version of the video.)

This video has been distributed widely both inside and outside the min-

ing industry. It is being used by many emergency rescue teams as a stark reminder of what can happen when the unexpected becomes a reality. The video was awarded a national Telly Award in 2003 (generally considered to be the "Oscar" for broadcast media such as TV, cable, and other commercial productions). *You Are My Sunshine* has been the most widely distributed of all the training videos produced, including to over 30 countries. It quickly reached an audience outside the mining industry and is being used in many other industries such as tunneling, firefighting, and the military. It has been aired repeatedly on the regional public TV station.

You Are My Sunshine was evaluated separately from the other NIOSH mine safety videos. This particular film was substantially different in nature from the others, and while responses to the evaluations did mention lessons learned, it became obvious that the film had touched a very personal place for many of the viewers. Because of the difference in audience and in the intent of those who showed the video, the analysis of *You Are My Sunshine* will not be included in this report, but will be reported in a separate document.

EVALUATION OF *ZEN AND THE ART OF ROCK BOLTING*

By Elaine T. Cullen and
Albert H. Fein

The seventh video produced under the NIOSH research project was entitled *Zen and the Art of Rock Bolting* (Cullen, 2002b) (figure 9). This video was made in response to an issue that was heard repeatedly from safety trainers across the country. Because workers in the mining industry in the United States are aging, the industry is anticipating a significant exodus of experienced miners within the next few years (Kowalski-Trakofler et al., 2004, p. 2). Some experts believe this is already happening. One of the results of the retirement of these master miners is that fewer mentors will be left to train the influx of new employees. In an industry that has relied heavily on the master-apprentice relationship for training new miners, this has the potential for disaster.

Figure 9.—*Zen and the Art of Rock Bolting* video poster.

Safety trainers are, quite reasonably, concerned about the situation. It is generally agreed that inexperienced workers have more than their share of accidents when compared to more experienced workers, particularly in blue-collar industries, and in an inherently dangerous industry such as mining, the number of accidents among new miners can run especially high. Consequently, trainers came to us with a question: Is it possible to capture the wisdom and expertise of a master miner and use these strengths to train new hires long after the master has left the mine? The *Zen* video is an attempt to answer that question.

Before filming could begin on this project, it was crucial to find a master miner who would be willing to work with us and who had the charisma to effectively teach what he knew while working in front of a camera. Jim Mortensen, a life-long veteran of the Sunshine Mine, filled these criteria. In the complicated world of the gypo miners, he was considered the best of the best. He had held the position of being the "top money man" at the Sunshine for nearly 37 years, and in spite of the fact that he was 58 when he agreed to work with the project, few miners at the mine believed they could out-mine him. Jim had the added trait of being a born storyteller with a wry sense of humor. Even though working on the film would slow him down and possibly keep him from "making the round" (thus denying him his bonus for the days we were working with him), he agreed to do it.

Robert Pirsig, in his book *Zen and the Art of Motorcycle Maintenance,* discusses what it is that makes the masters different.

Sometime look at a novice workman or a bad workman and compare his expression with that of a craftsman whose work you know is excellent and you'll see the difference. The craftsman isn't ever following a single line of instruction. He's making decisions as he goes along. For that reason he'll be absorbed and attentive to what he's doing even though he doesn't deliberately contrive this. His motions and the machine are in a kind of harmony. He isn't following any set of written instructions because the nature of the material at hand determines his thoughts and motions. (1974, p. 148)

This is a perfect description of a master miner at work. He is totally absorbed with his work, reading the environment constantly as he works, and making decisions about how he works as that environment changes. It was this mastery that we hoped to capture as we filmed Jim Mortensen at work.

By the time filming on the new video began, we had learned enough to know that it would be a waste of both our time and Jim's to script the story. Our plan was just to let him talk and demonstrate what he knew. Jim was very good at this, having trained more than his share of new hands over the years, but when we gave him a "new hire" to teach, he truly shone. The *Zen* video does not use the storytelling method employed in the other videos, although Jim does tell several stories. It is based only on what he would teach a new hire about how to stay alive in the mines long enough for him to become a good miner. Thus, Jim instructs his

new trainees in two important ways—through what he says and through what he does.

Fein, from the team of Fein and Isaacson that had assessed the effectiveness of the first five videos, was hired to evaluate *Zen*. During the initial stages of the first evaluation, the team determined that quantitative data collection methods did not provide the best means of assessing the effectiveness of the videos. The pre-test/post-test, true-false format designed for these videos was moderately successful in measuring trainees' knowledge of the content of each video, but it did not take into account how effectively the videos served as a reminder or reinforcement of knowledge that the miners already possessed but might not practice. The core question about each video was not really the amount of knowledge gained as measured by a true-false test, but how effectively the video affected miners' behavior. What

the evaluators concluded from the first set of video evaluations was that the information provided by the miners to the three open-ended questions at the end of the tests provided much more accurate and authentic data than did the more formal test questions.

Using answers to the open-ended questions as a guide, and with a greater understanding of the occupational culture of mining, Fein designed the evaluation instrument for *Zen* to be more open-ended, briefer, and less structured than the tests used for the other videos. In other words, this evaluation was designed to be qualitative in nature.

Creswell confirms the value of using qualitative methods when—

- The nature of the question begins with a "how" or "what."
- When the variables are not easily identified.
- When the topic calls for exploration.
- When the researcher is studying individuals in their natural setting. (1998, p. 17)

In the evaluation of *Zen*, the research questions to be answered were—

1. How effectively did *Zen and the Art of Rock Bolting* capture the wisdom and experience of a master miner? and

2. How effectively did *Zen and the Art of Rock Bolting* provide information to new and experienced min

Fein (2003) decided to again use a pre-viewing/post-viewing format for the evaluation, but with some significant differences to the instruments used for the evaluations of the first five videos. On the pre-test, only the following three questions were asked.

1. What needs to be done before a miner begins drilling or bolting?

2. What is important to remember about operating a jackleg?

3. What is important to miners who are working underground?

Additional questions were added to the post-test. The fourth question asked miners to write down anything they had learned from the video that hadn't been covered in the first three questions. The fifth question asked whether, after watching the video, the respondent would like Jim Mortensen to be his or her trainer. This question was meant to get at the efficacy of capturing a master miner on video and whether his expertise would be as evident if he were not there in person.

The trainers who participated in the pre-test also suggested adding a final question in which trainees were asked to choose whether the video had taught

an eye on. This was, in fact, the case. Post-test responses showed significant improvement over pre-test responses in both number of answers and completeness of answers and for both inexperienced and experienced miners. In addition, the majority of both inexperienced miners and experienced miners responded that the video taught them either "quite a bit" or "a lot." Comments from the inexperienced miners revealed the respect they had for a miner who had obviously mastered the art.

them "nothing," "a little," "quite a bit," or "a lot." As before, miners were also invited to provide any additional comments on the video. (See Appendix D for the final pre- and post-tests used to evaluate *Zen*.)

When the video was completed and approved, the mine safety community was notified via e-mail, *Technology News* mailings, the Website, and personal contacts. As before, the videos were free to safety trainers, but were sent only to those who requested them. Evaluation surveys were sent out with each video requested. Trainers were asked to administer the pre-test before showing the video and the post-test afterward. No verbal interview data were gathered from the trainers, although a separate questionnaire was sent to them to gather their thoughts on how effective the video was and whether they believed Jim's wisdom and expertise were obvious to the viewers (see Appendix E).

It was expected that after seeing the video, viewers would have more information and would thus provide more answers to the three open-ended questions about what miners should do and what things were important to keep

- You can only get so much from a video, but he does convey a lot of information. I could learn a lot from him.
- I think Jim would be an excellent teacher.
- I thought that this was one of the best training videos I have ever seen. I definitely would like to learn from Jim. He is not so formal or proper.
- Overall I enjoyed Jim. I think he was a very helpful teacher. It was nice to have a video where a person actually shows you how to do things instead of just tells you about it.
- Jim Mortensen would be a good teacher because he knows what he is talking about and explains it well.
- I think he was a good teacher because he has experienced everything there is to experience in a mine. He knows what to do and what can happen if you do something wrong. (Fein, 2003, p. 22)

---

[7]Details of the analysis of the evaluations are available in the report *Evaluation of Zen and the Art of Rock Bolting* (Fein, 2003).

In general, experienced miners, while recognizing the expert that Jim is, were more critical of the things they saw that were different than how they themselves mined. They were particularly critical of the safety violations they saw, even though Jim explains in the video that these were acceptable practices in the past but are no longer tolerated. The experienced miners recognized safety hazards and were vocal in their support for good safety practices.

- Very realistic...no sugar coating. While it is a good tool for training someone to be a productive bolter, safety was questionable.
- Very well done, but needs to watch some bad habits, like standing on the D ring.
- Obviously he knows his way around a mine and a jackleg.
- Good video with lots of good advice.
- He should use his glasses more. (Fein, 2003, p. 21)

Comments from the trainers concerning this video were also quite positive. They were asked to respond to whether or not they thought the video was an effective training tool and while three people did mention Jim's "bad habits," the others stated that the video was effective as a training tool.

- This video was effective as it shows the basics to miners who have never been around rock bolting.
- Effective. Experienced miner, one you would look up to, giving you advice. It was good having the young guy in the movie.
- Everyone liked it and would like to have Jim Mortensen be their instructor.
- It was an extremely effective video....I feel this real-world approach is a good way to go about promoting safety. Who better to hear it from than someone with years of experience?
- Showed actual practice. Noted some bad habits in addition to good ones.
- In general I have heard only positive reactions. We have had several dozen people view the film and every one of them have liked it. Yesterday four different miners said as how it was the best experienced-based effective film they had watched. Each experienced miner indicates that Jim is a true expert...a miner's miner. (pp. 23, 26)

Trainers were asked how they handled differences in policies or procedures between what Jim discussed or showed and what they expected at their mines. Most of them used the video as an opportunity to discuss those differences and to go over them. Where local policies differed from what was shown in *Zen*, it seemed easy for trainers to point out the difference and use them to clarify local standards and why they were set that way.

One of the more interesting things from the data analysis was that the post-test responses for inexperienced miners reflected a kind of "Aha!" for many of them. They had already heard many of the things that Jim discussed, but hearing them from an expert and watching him perform made the lessons much more meaningful. Learning

these things from a miner they saw as very credible enhanced their readiness to learn.

The two questions that the *Zen* video was seeking answers to were "whether or not it was possible to capture the wisdom and expertise of a master miner on film" and "whether a film of this type could effectively provide information to both new and experienced miners." From the responses gathered from both kinds of miners and the professional safety trainers, it would seem that the answer to both of these questions is "yes." If the right expert is found, a person who can share his wisdom and experiences with credibility and personality, it is possible to capture that expertise and use it to train future generations of miners.

SUMMARY AND CONCLUSIONS

By Elaine T. Cullen

The NIOSH research project "Development and Evaluation of Effective Safety Training for Miners" was designed to investigate what effective training tools would look like. Many social scientists have proposed theories about adult learning and the strong role that occupational culture plays in how, what, and why workers choose to learn. The popularity and positive attitude that the mining industry has toward the SRL/NIOSH videos proves that there is something to be learned from these theories. As adult learners, miners expect their training to be necessary, related to what they do in their work, and help them deal with the many environmental hazards and challenges they face on a daily basis. They also expect it to be interesting and enjoyable, even if it deals with technical topics. Miners have a greater need than many other workers to develop expertise, not just to absorb data from their training. The dynamic, dangerous nature of the work requires them to be able to draw on myriad lessons in order to survive. Effective training may play a critical role in that survival.

The mining industry has a long tradition of using a master-apprentice relationship in training new workers. These miner-mentors are effective because they are credible. They have learned their lessons through years of successfully surviving in an often-hostile underground environment. In addition, they talk and walk and act like miners. They are believable. A leading theorist, Albert Bandura, believes that this is a primary key to effective learning. New hires learn by listening to and

believing the stories told by older miners, and in doing so, they do not need to repeat those experiences (often "close calls" or worse) in order to learn. Storytelling, an age-old method of teaching new hires in the mining industry, is also an extremely effective means of conveying often-complex information in a way that is understandable and memorable. Storytelling has a crucial role to play in successful training.

A major factor in bringing about effective change in any culture is to work inside it, rather than to stand outside it. To truly change a person's behavior to incorporate a safer way of working, it is crucial that the locus of control be moved from external (the boss or the inspector who will punish unsafe behavior) to internal (the worker chooses the safe way to work because he/she realizes it is the better choice). Culture is the gatekeeper, however, and the filter through which all options are viewed. If training is provided by respected mentors who have been successful as miners and who understand the language and the norms of the mining culture, then training will be much more readily heard and adopted by the trainees, and they will make the choice to alter their behavior to be more like their mentors.

The training videos created by the SRL/NIOSH make use of the culturally acceptable constructs of miner-mentors, storytelling, and assurances that the lessons included are relevant as well as interesting. Evaluations of the videos have shown that they are valued by trainers and trainees alike because they are seen as credible and respectful of the mining culture. Viewers particularly appreciated the fact that the "actors" were real miners, and they were filmed do-

ing real mining activities in real operating mines. There are many ways to measure effectiveness of training materials, but the fact that trainers report that their miners are asking for the NIOSH videos and that they discuss them for weeks after seeing them is an indication that the miners paid attention. One surprising result of this interest is that many trainers are reporting that the videos are disappearing from training rooms. Miners, it seems, are "borrowing" them and taking them home to show their families.

SRL will continue to evaluate the training videos it produces. Much has been learned about how to do this in a meaningful way, and these lessons will be applied to the development of future effective training products.

REFERENCES

Billett, S. (1994). *Situated learning in the workplace: Having another look at apprenticeships. Industrial and Commercial Training,* 26(11), 9-16.

Bruner, J. (1990). *Acts of meaning.* Cambridge, MA: Harvard University Press.

Camm, T. W., & Cullen, E. T. (2002). *Releasing the energy of workers to create a safer workplace: The value of using mentors to enhance safety training.* In R. H. Peters (Ed.), *Strategies for improving miners' training* (Information Circular 9463, pp. 35-38). Pittsburgh, PA: National Institute for Occupational Safety and Health.

Caudron, S. (2000). *Learners speak out. Training & Development,* 54(4), 52-57.

Cole, H. P. (1997). *Stories to live by: A narrative approach to health-behavior research and injury prevention.* In D. S. Gochman (Ed.), *Handbook of health behavior research methods:* Vol. 4 (pp. 325-349). New York: Plenum.

Cranton, P. (1994). *Understanding and promoting transformative learning: A guide for educators of adults.* San Francisco: Jossey-Bass.

Creswell, J. W. (1998). *Qualitative inquiry and research design: Choosing among five traditions.* Thousand Oaks, CA: Sage.

Cullen, E. T. (Producer and Director) (1999). *Explosives underground - Handling explosives in modern mines.* Video. Spokane, WA: Spokane Research Laboratory/NIOSH.

Cullen, E. T. (Producer and Director) (2000). *Miner Mike saves the day - or- Ground support, it's important.* Video. Spokane, WA: Spokane Research Laboratory/NIOSH.

Cullen, E. T. (Producer and Director) (2001a). *Hazards in motion.* Video. Spokane, WA: Spokane Research Laboratory/NIOSH.

Cullen, E. T. (Producer and Director) (2001b). *Hidden scars.* Video. Spokane, WA: Spokane Research Laboratory/NIOSH.

Cullen, E. T. (Producer and Director) (2002a). *You are my Sunshine.* Video. Spokane, WA: Spokane Research Laboratory/NIOSH.

Cullen, E. T. (Producer and Director) (2002b). *Zen and the Art of Rock Bolting.* Video. Spokane, WA: Spokane Research Laboratory/NIOSH.

Darwin, A. (2000). *Critical reflections on mentoring in work settings. Adult Education Quarterly,* 50(3), 197-211.

Fein, A. H. (2003) *Evaluation of Zen and the Art of Rock Bolting.* Report prepared for the Spokane Research Laboratory, Spokane, WA. 38 pp.

Fein, A. H., & Isaacson, N. S. (2001). *Video-based training program for underground miners evaluation report.* Report prepared for the Spokane Research Laboratory, Spokane, WA. 105 pp.

Forster, N., Cebis, M., Majteles, S., Mathur, A., Morgan, R., Preuss, J., & Tiwar, V. (1999). *The role of story-telling in organizational leadership. Leadership & Organizational Development Journal,* 20(1).

Gargiulo, T. L. (2002). *Making stories: A practical guide to organizational leaders and human response specialists.* Westport, CT: Quorum Books.

Geertz, C. (1973). *The interpretation of cultures: Selected essays by Clifford Geertz.* New York: Basic Books.

Hansen, C. D. (1995). *Occupational cultures: Whose frame are we using? Journal for Quality and Participation,* 18(3), 60-64.

Hofstede, G. (1997). *Cultures and organizations: Software of the mind.* New York: McGraw-Hill.

Jerome, T. *Personal communication,* February 2002.

King, J., & Down, J. (2001). *On taking stories seriously: Emotional and moral intelligences. Teaching Business Ethics,* 5(4), 419-437.

Kirkpatrick, D. (2001). *The four-level evaluation process.* In L. L. Ukens (Ed.), *What smart trainers know: The secrets of success from the world's foremost experts* (pp. 122-132). San Francisco: Jossey-Bass/Pfeiffer.

Knowles, M. S., Holton, E. F., & Swanson, R. A. (1998). *The adult learner* (5th ed.). Woburn, MA: Butterworth-Heinemann.

Kowalski, K. M., & Vaught, C. (2002). *Principles of adult learning: Application for mine trainers.* In R. H. Peters (Ed.), *Strategies for improving miners' training* (Information Circular 9463, pp. 3-8). Pittsburgh, PA: National Institute for Occupational Safety and Health.

Kowalski-Trakofler, K., Vaught, C., Mallett, L., Brnich, M., Reinke, D., Steiner, L., Wiehagen, W., & Rethi, L. (eds.), (2004). *Safety and health training for an evolving workforce: An overview from the mining industry* (Information Circular 9474). Pittsburgh, PA: National Institute for Occupational Safety and Health.

Lave, J., & Wenger, E. (1991). *Situated learning: Legitimate peripheral participation.* Cambridge, UK: Cambridge University Press.

Livo, N. J., & Rietz, S. A. (1986). *Storytelling: Process and practice.* Littleton, CO: Libraries Unlimited, Inc.

Lucas, R. A. (1969). *Men in crisis: A study of a mine disaster.* New York: Basic Books.

MacDonald, M. R. (1993). *The story-teller's start-up book: Finding, learning, performing and using folktales.* Little Rock, AR: August House.

Mallett, L., & Reinke, D. (2002). *An overview of the evaluation process for mine trainers.* In R. H. Peters (Ed.), *Strategies for improving miners' training* (Information Circular 9463, pp. 13-17). Pittsburgh, PA: National Institute for Occupational Safety and Health.

McCarl, R. (1997). Contested space: *The above and below ground landscape of Idaho's Coeur d'Alene Mining District.* Salt Lake City: University of Utah Graduate School of Architecture.

Miller, A. (Producer and Director) (1999). *Preventing rock falls in underground mines.* Video. Spokane, WA: Spokane Research Laboratory/NIOSH.

Miller, A., Oaks, M. M., Akmal, T. T. (1998). *Criteria and rationale for development of a video based training program for underground miners.* Internal report, Spokane, WA: National Institute for Occupational Safety and Health.

Miller, P. (1993). *Theories of Developmental Psychology* . New York: W. H. Freeman.

Mitchell, B. *Personal communication,* February 2001.

Neuhauser, P. C. (1993). *Corporate legends & lore.* Austin, TX: PCN Associates.

Owenby, P. H. (1992). *Making case studies come alive. Training,* 29(1), 43-47.

Patton, M. Q. (2002). *Qualitative research and evaluation methods.* Thousand Oaks, CA: Sage.

Pegg, M. (1999). *The art of mentoring. Industrial and Commercial Training,* 31(4), 136-141.

Pirsig, R. M. (1974). *Zen and the art of motorcycle maintenance.* New York: Bantam New Age Books.

Schein, E. H. (1996). *Culture: The missing concept in organization studies. Administrative Science Quarterly,* 41(2), 229-239.

Simmons, A. (2001). *The story factor: Inspiration, influence, and persuasion through the art of storytelling.* Cambridge, MA: Perseus Publishing.

Slater, M. D. (2002). *Entertainment education and the persuasive impact of narratives.* In T. Brock, J. J. Strange, & M. C. Green (Eds.), *Narrative impact: Social and cognitive foundations.* Hillsdale, NJ: Erlbaum.

Stone, D. (1999) S*ocial cognitive theory [Web Page].* *URL www.med.usf.edu/Ekmbrown/Social_Cognitive_Theory_Overview.htm.*

U.S. Code of Federal Regulations, Title 30 CFR Part 46.4, 30 CFR 46 & 48, 30 CFR 56/57/58, (2001). *Federal Metal and Nonmetal Mine Safety, Health & Training Regulations.*

Van Maanen, J., & Barley, S. R. (1984). *Occupational communities: Culture and control in organizations.* In Staw & Cummings (Eds.), *Research in organizational behavior: Vol. 6* (pp. 287-366). Greenwich, CT: JAI Press.

Voynick, S. M. (1978). *The making of a hardrock miner.* Kearney, NE: Morris Publishing.

Whyatt, J., Williams, T., & White, B. (2000). *Ground conditions and the May 13, 1994 rock burst, Coeur d'Alene Mining District, northern Idaho.* In J. Girard, M. Leibman, C. Breeds, & T. Doe (Eds.), *Pacific rocks 2000: Rocks around the rim: Proceedings of the 4th North American rock mechanics symposium* (pp. 313-318). Rotterdam: Balkema.

Wlodowski, R. J. (1985). *Enhancing adult motivation to learn.* San Francisco: Jossey-Bass.

Wylie, A. (1998). *Story telling: A powerful form of communication. Communication World,* 15(3), 30-32.

Zemke, R. (1990). *Storytelling: Back to a basic. Training,* 27(3), 44-50.

Zemke, R. (2002). *Who needs learning theory anyway? Training,* 39(9), 86-91.

APPENDIX A

Zen and the Art of Rock Bolting

Technical Review

The purpose of this video is to "capture the wisdom and knowledge of the expert miner before he leaves the industry". How well do you think this was done?

The primary audience for this video is young miners. Do you think it is an appropriate training tool for new hands?

Do you think there is value in the video for reminding more experienced miners?

Does this video generally demonstrate acceptable practices?

What do you think of the idea of using experienced miners to help train others? Is this an effective training technique?

What topics do you think would be valuable for additional "expert miner" videos?

Additional comments?

APPENDIX B

Hazards in Motion

Pretest

I am: A new miner (less than one year)_____ An experienced miner _____

DIRECTIONS:
Circle the letter of the correct response.

1. Which is NOT necessary before operating mine vehicles?
    A. Check to see if the lights and brakes work.
    B. Check to see if the fuel, transmission fluid, and oil levels are okay.
    C. Check the tires for proper inflation.
    D. Check fire extinguisher(s) dates and to see if they've been used.
    E. None of the above

2. When using LHDs
    A. Pedestrians must yield.
    B. Hang on with both hands when riding in the bucket.
    C. Drive with the bucket downward behind the vehicle.
    D. Watch out for pinch points
    E. Drive as fast or slowly as you want.

3. Which is NOT true about working in mines?
    A. A head lamp moving up and down means "back up."
    B. A head lamp moving side to side means "stop."
    C. Horseplay and joking around help break the tedium.
    D. Always check with the person in charge of a work zone before entering it.
    E. There may be red and green traffic signals.

4. Which is NOT true about rail cars?
    A. Will have trip lights on the last car if it's pulling or on the first car if it's pushing.
    B. Block wheel if parking the cars
    C. Can be used to carry a few tools and equipment if not a mantrip.
    D. Have locomotive cars that are convenient for carrying small tools.
    E. Operators can't see ahead easily.

5. When using mine elevators
    A. Always wear safety glasses.
    B. Wait a minimum of five feet from the shaft.
    C. Lock both latches after closing the cage door.
    D. Keep hands (and other body parts) inside the cage at all times.
    E. Establish a solid footing because the cages moves quickly.

Hazards in Motion

Posttest

I am: A new miner (less than one year)_____ An experienced miner _____

DIRECTIONS:
Mark T if the statement is TRUE and F if the statement is FALSE

_____ 1. Before operating mine vehicles check to see if the lights and brakes work.

_____ 2. Before operating mine vehicles check the transmission fluid, oil, and fuel levels.

_____ 3. Before operating mine vehicles check fire extinguishers to see if they've been used and the date.

_____ 4. Before operating mine vehicles check the tires for proper inflation

_____ 5. When using LHDs ignore pinch points.

_____ 6. The best place to ride in an LHD is in the bucket.

_____ 7. When using LHDs the bucket should be in front of the vehicle.

_____ 8. LHDs have the right of way over pedestrians.

_____ 9. LHDs may be operated at any speed.

_____ 10. Mines often have red and green traffic signals--just like streets.

_____ 11. A head lamp moving side to side means "stop."

_____ 12. A head lamp moving up and down means "come ahead."

_____ 13. A head lamp moving up and down means "back up."

_____ 14. Always check with the person in charge of a work zone before entering it.

_____ 15. Horseplay and joking around in mines is OK because they help break the tedium.

_____ 16. Rail cars always have the right of way.

_____ 17. People and equipment should be carried in separate cars.

_____ 18. The locomotive is a convenient spot to carry small tools.

_____ 19 Locomotive operators sit up high and therefore generally have good visibility of the track ahead.

_____ 20. Always wear safety glasses when using mine elevators.

_____ 21 When waiting for the elevator, stand 15 feet from the shaft.

_____ 22. Lock both latches after closing the cage door.

_____ 23. Establish a solid footing in a mine elevator because the cage moves quickly.

_____ 24. Always block wheels if parking a vehicle.

_____ 25. When rail cars are coupling, use a coupling device to avoid injury.

_____ 26. When uncoupling rail cars, beware of pinch points.

_____ 27. Air doors should be left open for proper air circulation in the mine.

_____ 28. When mine cars are dumped, stand near the grizzly to make sure they empty properly.

_____ 29. Signal the hoistman when you are ready to exit the mine elevator.

_____ 30. Never operate any equipment you have not been trained to operate.

PLEASE GIVE US SOME FEEDBACK ON THIS VIDEO

(Circle the NUMBER that best describes YOU)

Hazards in Motion taught me something I did not know:
NO 1 2 3 4 5 YES

Hazards in Motion "talked down" to me:
NO 1 2 3 4 5 YES

Hazards in Motion was enjoyable to watch:
NO 1 2 3 4 5 YES

Comments:

Miner Mike Saves the Day

Pretest

I am: A new miner (less than one year) _____   An experienced miner _____

DIRECTIONS Part I:
Circle the letter of the correct response.

1. Which is NOT a reason that rocks may fail?
    A. Cooling hot lines increase rock stress.
    B. Blasting loosens the rock.
    C. Over-barring down.
    D. Exposure to air dries out the rock.

2. Which is NOT true about scaling rock?
    A. Use the right length bar.
    B. Stay in safe ground.
    C. Pay attention to where the rock will fall.
    D. Bar in any direction.

3. Which is NOT true about operating a jack-leg
    A. Let the bolt extend no more than six inches from the surface.
    B. Barring down is unnecessary.
    C. Look at the ground to determine how many bolts are needed.
    D. Keep the machine leg balanced and in line with the drilling surface.

4. Which is NOT true about operating a jumbo bolter?
    A. Keep the area clear of tools and debris.
    B. Always use a scaling bar before operating the machine.
    C. Turn off the machine at the first sight of rock movement.
    D. None of the above.

5. Which is NOT true about jumbo drills and rock bolters?
    A. Are not as safe as jack drills.
    B. Should be operated slowly in muddy ground.
    C. Require the operator to use judgment.
    D. Provide protection under unbolted areas.

6. When installing mechanicals
    A. Check tightness with a torque wrench.
    B. Never use expanding anchors.
    C. Any size bit will do.
    D. Never drill the hole too short.

7. Bolts
    A. Should be installed only according to the design plan.
    B. Increase ground support.
    C. Sometimes are used with plywood.
    D. Usually have metal plates at the bottom.

DIRECTIONS Part II:
Mark "T" of the statement is TRUE and "F" if the statement is FALSE or PAR-
TIALLY FALSE.

_____1. It is more important to be safe than to make the round.

_____2. Skipping a few bolts saves time and does no real harm.

_____3. Most mines use the same kind of ground support.

_____4. Following the company's bolt design plan will guarantee safe working conditions.

_____5. There can be quite a bit of variation in ground conditions.

_____6. There is more tension when the rock is pulled than when it is compressed.

_____7. Blasting rock changes ground conditions by increasing tension.

_____8. Point anchor bolts and grouter bolts with plates are active supports.

_____9. Installing passive bolts puts the rock back into tension.

_____10. Grouted cable bolts and grouter bolts without plates are active supports.

_____11. Passive supports prevent additional relation of the rock from occurring.

_____12. A properly installed bolt creates a zone of compressed rock.

_____13. Leaving out one bolt is dangerous.

_____14. Miners have to use their own judgment about how many bolts to install.

_____15. Barring down takes time but makes installing bolts safer.

_____16. Once a miner has scaled, it is safe to install bolts and it won't be
      necessary to scale again.

_____17. Friction bolts are most suitable for broken ground.

_____18. The bolt design plan represents the maximum number of bolts that are
      safe to install.

_____19. The only way to stabilize rock is to use timbers, bolts, or steel sets.

_____20. The best way to keep track of dangerous situations when using a jumbo bolter is to listen for strange or unusual sounds.

_____21. Safety glasses are a must when using the scaling bar.

_____22. If you see faults or seams, consider using shorter bolts.

_____23. Grouted bolts that use resin should be drilled fairly deep.

_____24. Once a bolt that uses resin or cement is set, the bolt should not spin.

_____25. Use wire mesh or welded wire panels to make breaking ground safer.

_____26. Once bolts, wire mesh, timbers, or other safety measures are installed, miners can relax and be safe.

_____27. A wire mesh properly bolted and full of broken rock is safe.

_____28. If a bolt has pulled through the plate, enough compression is maintained to insure safe conditions.

_____29. Broken rock on the floor of the mine just means someone didn't clean up their area.

_____30. If you see signs of failing ground, and you have the right tools, you should repair the problem immediately.

Miner Mike Saves the Day

Posttest

I am: A new miner (less than one year) _____ An experienced miner _____

DIRECTIONS:
Mark "T" of the statement is TRUE and "F" if the statement is FALSE or PAR-TIALLY FALSE.

_____1. It is more important to be safe than to make the round.

_____2. Skipping a few bolts saves time and does no real harm.

_____3. Most mines use the same kind of ground support.

_____4. Following the company's bolt design plan will guarantee safe working conditions.

_____5. There can be quite a bit of variation in ground conditions.

_____6. There is more tension when the rock is pulled than when it is compressed.

_____7. Blasting rock changes ground conditions by increasing tension.

_____8. Point anchor bolts and grouter bolts with plates are active supports.

_____9. Installing passive bolts puts the rock back into tension.

_____10. Grouted cable bolts and grouter bolts without plates are active supports.

_____11. Passive supports prevent additional relation of the rock from occurring.

_____12. A properly installed bolt creates a zone of compressed rock.

_____13. Leaving out one bolt isn't very dangerous.

_____14. Miners have to use their own judgment about how many bolts to install.

_____15. Barring down takes time but makes installing bolts safer.

_____16. Once a miner has scaled, it is safe to install bolts and it won't be necessary to scale again.

_____17. Friction bolts are most suitable for broken ground

_____18. A bolt design plan represents the maximum number of bolts that are safe to install.

_____19. The only ways to stabilize rock are to use timbers, bolts, or steel sets.

_____20. The best way to keep track of dangerous situations when using a jumbo bolter is to listen for strange or unusual sounds.

_____21. Safety glasses are a must when using the scaling bar.

_____22. If you see faults or seams, consider using shorter bolts.

_____23. Grouted bolts that use resin should be drilled fairly deep.

_____24. Once a bolt that uses resin or cement is set, the bolt should not spin.

_____25. Use wire mesh or welded wire panels to make breaking ground safer.

_____26. Once bolts, wire mesh, timbers, or other safety measures are installed, miners can relax and be safe.

_____27. A wire mesh properly bolted and full of broken rock is safe.

_____28. If a bolt has pulled through the plate, enough compression is maintained to insure safe conditions.

_____29. Broken rock on the floor of the mine just means someone didn't clean up.

_____30. If you see signs of failing ground, and you have the right tools, you should repair the problem immediately.

_____31. Rocks may fail because cooling hot lines increase rock stress.

_____32. Over-barring down loosens the rock and increases stress.

_____33. Exposure to air dries out the rock and may cause increased stress.

_____34. When scaling rock, the length of the bar used doesn't really matter.

_____35. Never bar downward; only upward.

_____36. When operating a jack-leg, let the bolt extend no more than six inches from the surface.

_____37. Keep a jack-leg balanced and in line with the drilling surface.

_____38. When operating a jumbo bolter turn off the machine at the first sight of rock movement.

_____39. Jumbo drills are not as safe as jack drills.

_____40. Because of their design, jumbo drills provide protection under unbolted areas

_____41. When installing mechanicals use expanding anchors and the right sized bit.

_____42. For added safety, check tightness of the first and last mechanical you install with a torque wrench.

_____43. Never drill the hole too short when installing bolts.

_____44. Bolts usually have metal or wood plates at the bottom to increase ground support.

PLEASE GIVE US SOME FEEDBACK ON THIS VIDEO

(Circle the NUMBER that best describes YOU)

Miner Mike taught me something I did not know:
NO 1 2 3 4 5 YES

Miner Mike "talked down" to me:
NO 1 2 3 4 5 YES

Miner Mike was enjoyable to watch:
NO 1 2 3 4 5 YES

Comments:

APPENDIX C

Hidden Scars

Pretest

I am:
A new miner (less than one year experience)_____
An experienced miner_____

There are no "right" answers to these questions:

Imagine yourself in a mine disaster. Your co-workers are hurt or worse. You are trapped in fallen earth.

What might be your thoughts and feelings?

You survive, but how might such an experience impact you?

your family?

Your community?

Hidden Scars

Posttest

I am:

A new miner (less than one year experience_____)

An experienced miner_____

There are no "right" answers to these questions:

You have just watched a video about a mine disaster that caused injury and a fatality.

1. What are your thoughts and feelings about what you saw and heard?

2. What did you learn from watching this video?

3. In what way(s) will this video impact your work?

Please give us some feedback on this video
(Circle the NUMBER that best describes YOU.)

Hidden Scars taught me something I did not know:
NO   1   2   3   4   5   YES

Hidden Scars "talked down" to me:
NO   1   2   3   4   5   YES

Hidden Scars was enjoyable to watch:
NO   1   2   3   4   5   YES

Comments:

APPENDIX D

Zen and the Art of Rockbolting

BEFORE VIEWING THE VIDEO

NAME

How long have you been a miner?
_____Less than 1 year
_____1 to 3 years
_____Longer than 3 years

DIRECTIONS:

In "Zen and the Art of Rockbolting," Jim Mortensen describes how to get mining work done **efficiently** and **safely.** Early in the video Jim says "There's always ten ways to do one job." Given that, there are many possible right answers to the questions that follow. **For every question, imagine that you are the expert talking to a complete novice.**

1. What needs to be done before a miner begins drilling or bolting?

2. What is important to remember about operating a jackleg?

3. What is important to miners who are working underground?

Zen and the Art of Rockbolting

NAME   **How long have you been a miner?**
_____Less than 1 year
_____1 to 3 years
_____Longer than 3 years

DIRECTIONS:
Add any **additional information** that would help a new miner be more efficient or safer. You may **refer back to what you wrote** BEFORE VIEWING THE VIDEO, but **do NOT repeat what you wrote on the first page.** Use the back of this page if necessary

1. What needs to be done before a miner begins drilling or bolting?

2. What is important to remember about operating a jackleg?

3. What is important to miners when working at the face?

4. Write anything else you learned from the video that isn't already written above.

5. Would you like Jim to be your trainer?

CIRCLE ONE: The video taught me: Nothing   A little   Quite a bit   A Lot

Your comments about "Zen and the Art of Rockbolting":

APPENDIX E

Zen and the Art of Rockbolting

TRAINER'S QUESTIONNAIRE

1.   In general, what were your reactions to the video? Was it an effective training tool? Why or why not?

2.   Methods of operation vary from mine to mine. Did you address any differences in your mine's operation from Jim's ways? Would these differences get in the way of using the video for training again?

3.   What materials could accompany this video that would make it a more effective training tool for you?

4.   Does Jim Mortensen come across as an expert? Is he credible as a teacher? Why or why not?

5.   Would you like to see NIOSH produce additional "Expert Miner" type videos? If so, on what topics?